COMPUTER PROGRAMMING/FORTRAN

The modern digital computer is capable of carrying out more than one million operations a second, each of which it has to be instructed to perform. The list of instructions telling the computer what to do is called a program and is written in special computer language.

It is not difficult for a person with some knowledge of arithmetic and algebra to learn to program a computer using one of the high-level programming languages currently available. This book provides a basic course in the Fortran language, widely adopted for scientific and general-purpose use. After outlining the development of the digital computer and computer languages, the author discusses flowcharts, the technique whereby the sequence of events to be performed in solving a problem is established. He then examines some of the basic ideas and principles of Fortran, and looks at the punched card and methods of specifying what arithmetical operations are to be performed. Control statements and input and output devices are next discussed, and examples of programs given. Further chapters cover subprograms, other features of Fortran that the programmer is likely to encounter and some of the other computer languages available. Exercises are included in most chapters, the answers to which are given at the end of the book.

TEACH YOURSELF BOOKS

COMPUTER PROGRAMMING/ FORTRAN

Arthur S. Radford
B.Sc., M.Sc., F.B.C.S.
Principal Lecturer in Computer Science,
Leicester Polytechnic

ST PAUL'S HOUSE WARWICK LANE
LONDON EC4P 4AH

First printed 1975

ISBN 0 340 19495 2

Printed and bound in Great Britain
for The English Universities Press Ltd
by Richard Clay (The Chaucer Press), Ltd, Bungay, Suffolk

Contents

Preface

There can be very few people in the developed countries now who have never heard of the computer. It influences our everyday life enormously. The banks have come so to rely upon it that our economic system would be in grave danger of collapse if all the computers were suddenly to stop working. The probability is that the majority of your monthly bills are prepared by a computer. These machines are not distant 'electronic brains' with which we have little contact—they are with us and among us now. It follows that we should know a little about them, their capabilities, the things they can and cannot do. If the clerk behind the counter blames the mistake in your account on the computer, do you believe him? After reading this book, you may have reservations.

It is not difficult for a person of average intelligence and some interest in problem-solving to learn to program a modern computer, using one of the many high-level programming languages currently available. The purpose of this book is to provide a brief course in the more important features of the popular Fortran language, assuming no prior knowledge of the digital computer. A slight acquaintance with arithmetic and algebra is desirable. CSE or GCE 'O' level is quite adequate in the United Kingdom, the normal school leaving standard elsewhere.

A. S. Radford
1974

1 Introduction

Progress and increased efficiency in many different fields has led, in many cases, to the need to be able to do more and more arithmetic quickly and accurately. In science, many problems have been left unsolved in the past just because the amount of calculation needed was so great that no individual, or team of individuals, was capable of performing it in the time available. In commercial fields, too, methods and practices long known to be inefficient have had to be tolerated, on the grounds that improved methods would need far too much calculation to be practical if such calculations had to be done by hand.

These problems have been realised almost from the time at which man first started to count and to appreciate the power and use of numbers. He has continually sought ways to make arithmetic easier and faster. The human brain is a wonderful computer, but the rate at which a man, unaided, can do arithmetic is pitifully slow by comparison with that of modern equipment. On the other hand, the rate at which the brain can absorb, store and retrieve information is much superior to that of any present-day machine.

Man has always tried to augment his natural calculating ability by one means or another. At first he must have counted on his fingers, which probably explains why our most commonly used number system is based on the number 10. Later, primitive calculating devices such as the abacus appeared, the efficiency and ease of use of which may be judged from the fact that it is still in use all over the world. The slide rule and desk calculating machines, the advent of the punched card and the transistor all led inevitably to the modern electronic digital computer which has brought about such a revolution in computing methods over the last twenty-five years or so.

The idea of a machine which would automatically perform a series of arithmetic operations is not a new one. Charles Babbage (1792–1871) built what could probably be described as the first computer, though the digits of the numbers manipulated were represented by the positions of a toothed wheel rather than, as they are today, by electrical or magnetic impulses. Babbage's Analytical Engine embodied in its design many of the principles of the modern computer, but its construction—begun in 1833—was never completed because of the difficulties of making the parts to the required precision.

The electronic digital computer

It was not until the end of World War II that the first true electronic computers appeared, and these machines were very different from the equipment which we use today. Rarely has an industry developed in such a brief space of time or have new techniques been perfected so rapidly as in the case of the digital computer. The first machine, ENIAC (Electronic Numerical Integrator And Calculator), which represented a tremendous step forward, was little more than a toy by comparison with today's machines, many of which are capable of performing more than a million operations per second.

Very early on, it was realised that to make the best use of the very high speed with which a computer can perform arithmetic it is necessary to keep operator intervention to a minimum. For instance, one might organise the operation of a computer such that the operator were required to type one instruction at a time, which the machine would then act upon and wait for the next instruction, and so on. Such a system would be very wasteful, since any operator, no matter how skilled, would inevitably be much slower in his actions than the computer. Consequently, the machine would stand idle for much of the time waiting for new instructions. Some of the earliest computers did work on a principle similar to this, and a great deal of operator intervention was necessary.

The next step was the introduction of the *stored-program* computer. In this machine, the list of instructions telling the computer what it is to do (the *program*) is first stored away inside the computer, which *reads* the program from punched cards or paper tape and then holds the information in its *memory*, or *store*. The ability to store a program in this way is a very real advantage, and the information can be read very quickly by modern punched card and paper tape readers linked to the computer. The computer does not now have to wait for human intervention after it has performed each instruction, because the next instruction is already in the machine and can be selected automatically. This technique also permits more complicated programs to be executed, because the machine can be instructed to repeat specified groups of instructions as many times as may be necessary, thus allowing repeated calculations of the same type.

One example of such repetition occurs in the calculation of weekly wages for a firm employing a large number of workers. A computer can do this job very well, but the task becomes impractical if the program which specifies the calculation has to be re-entered into the computer for each worker. When the program is stored in the memory of the machine, the calculations can be repeated by using the same sequence of instructions over again, entering new data for each man in turn.

The early 1950s saw the commercial introduction of the stored-program computer—the so-called 'first-generation' machines which were produced for the next eight or nine years before giving way to the faster and more economical 'second-generation' machines. These used transistor circuitry, a great advance which led into the current 'third generation' of machines using integrated circuit techniques. Writing programs for these earlier machines was, in general, more difficult than the programming of modern machines. This, in turn, limited the extent of the problems which could be handled by first-generation machines, though a great deal of very important work was completed and many new techniques were developed during this period.

The main difficulty was that it was necessary to write programs in what is known as *machine language* or *machine code*. This is the most basic and detailed form of programming, and requires that the programmer give explicit instructions to the machine for every operation to be performed, even the most fundamental. It is necessary, for example, to state exactly where the machine shall store the numbers it is to use; where they are to be found for some precisely defined arithmetic process; where the result of each intermediate calculation is to be held, and a host of other fiddling details. In addition, it might be necessary to express the instructions in a numerical code, and the numbers used would quite possibly be in some number system other than the decimal system, based on 10, with which we are most familiar. At worst, we might be obliged to use the binary system, based on 2, in which, for instance, the number 123 is expressed as 1111011.

The form of machine language differs from machine to machine, since it depends on the design of the particular machine. This means that programs written in the machine language of one computer cannot usually be executed on any other machine except one of exactly the same type as the first. It follows that a great deal of work must be duplicated, and the problem is particularly serious when a new computer of a different type is installed. A further implication is that if a person has learnt to program one computer, he is likely to have to spend a lot of time re-learning when a new computer is introduced.

Another disadvantage of machine language programming

is that it is a specialist business, and the originator of a problem is unlikely to have the necessary skill to be able to express its solution in the form of a machine language program. This can be a great disadvantage, for the programmer is, equally, likely to be ignorant of the field to which the problem applies. Thus a communication barrier appears, and this also can be serious where frequent changes to the program are required or there is a rapid turnover in programming staff, as often happens.

There thus appeared a need to make programming languages more easily learnt, and to make programs transferable from one computer to others of different types. It was necessary to raise the 'level' of the language used to express the program above that of the basic machine code to something rather more like that used by mathematicians or those engaged in commerce.

One of the first steps towards this goal was the introduction of the *subroutine*—a small program, permanently stored in the computer's memory, designed to perform automatically certain basic arithmetic or logical operations—the sorting of a set of numbers, for example, or the extraction of the square root of a number. Most computer systems had available a library of subroutines which could be made use of by the programmers, who were thus saved a great deal of detailed coding. To extract the square root of a number, for example, one would place the number in a specified position in memory, write a single instruction to 'call' the square root subroutine, and the result would appear in some other memory position.

The use of the subroutine led eventually to the development of languages called *autocodes*, which greatly simplified programming. Autocode instructions were similar in appearance to simple algebraic expressions. The following are examples:

A = 2 B = 3.6 C = A+B

No basic change in the nature of the computer had occurred. Each machine continued to recognise only its own machine language. The autocode instructions presented to the computer had to be translated into its machine language before they could be executed. But the process of translation could be specified exactly by a computer program written in machine language, and so translation from autocode to machine language could be performed automatically *by the computer itself*. The sequence of events is shown diagrammatically in Fig. 1.1

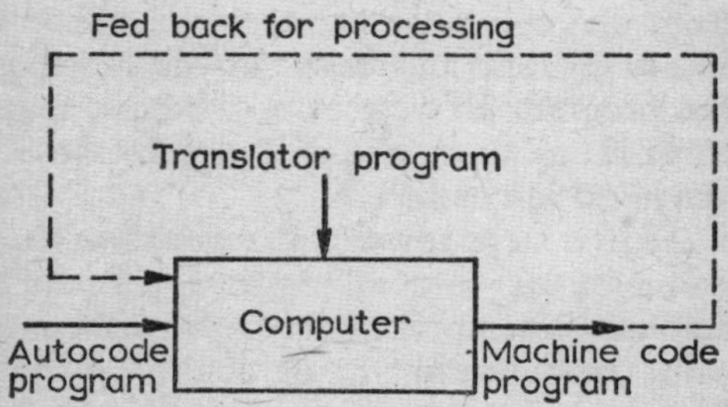

Fig. 1.1

The machine language instructions resulting from the translation were fed back into the machine, which could now recognise them and act accordingly. The writing of such a translation program is a very involved job, requiring an extensive knowledge of the computer concerned and a lot of skill.

The problem of machine-dependence remained, however, for autocodes were generally designed with a particular machine or group of machines in mind, and programs written for one machine were still likely to be unusable on a different type without extensive modification. However, they were at least more readable, and the task of rewriting was thereby made somewhat less of a chore. The problem of machine-dependence of computer programs is with us still, though we are much further advanced in the field of language design, and transfer of programs from computer to computer is now much easier than it used to be.

Fortran

Soon after the appearance of the autocodes came the first of what are now generally known as the 'high-level' languages. It was developed in the United States by the International Business Machines Corporation (IBM), and quickly adopted by the manufacturers of other equipment as a general-purpose computer language, largely independent of the machine on which it was to be used. The name given to this language was FORTRAN, an acronym for FORmula TRANslator, and it has become one of the most widely adopted computer languages for scientific and general-purpose use. The arrival of Fortran heralded a new era in computer programming, for it enabled programs to be expressed in a way which is very similar to that used in everyday mathematical notation.

The following oversimplified problem should give an idea of the appearance of a Fortran program. Suppose that it is required to convert a number of lengths given in feet to their equivalent lengths expressed in miles. If B is a representation of any length expressed in feet, and A represents the corresponding length in miles, we may write a formula connecting B and A, as follows:

A = B/5280.0

where the symbol / is used to denote division and 5280.0 is the number of feet in a mile.

The formula given above is, in fact, an 'instruction' in the Fortran language, though it is perhaps more commonly referred to as a *statement*. However, it indicates only the way in which one length may be converted, and it is not usually economically practical to use a computer for such a small problem. Let us be a little more realistic and assume that there are 5000 such lengths to be converted. The basic process for a computer program would be to read a length value (in feet) into the computer, perform the conversion calculation, print out the result, and repeat the set of operations another 4999 times. The following is a Fortran program which could be used to achieve this.

```
  DO 1 J=1,5000
  READ(2,2) B
  A = B/5280.0
1 WRITE(3,3) B,A
  STOP
2 FORMAT(F10.0)
3 FORMAT(10X, 2F8.3)
  END
```

This will look rather strange to the uninitiated, but it is a complete set of instructions to the computer for the performance of 5000 calculations. The first statement tells the machine to DO what follows, up to and including the statement labelled 1, 5000 times. This includes READing the value B, calculating the value A, and WRITing out the values of B and A. STOP is self-explanatory. The FORMAT statements, labelled 2 and 3, are used to indicate how the data are laid out on the punched card used to present information to the computer, and how the results are to be arranged on the printed page, and the END statement indicates the physically last statement of the program. All these statements, and a number of others, will be dealt with in the chapters that follow.

It will be seen that English words and phrases are used, together with conventional mathematical symbols, and the user of Fortran needs to know very little about the computer which he will be using. Again, the computer will be able to recognise only its own machine language, and so the Fortran program will have to be translated into that language. This translation process is referred to as *compilation*, and the program which accomplishes it is usually known as a *compiler*.

Not surprisingly, manufacturers other than IBM produced their own high-level programming languages which were similar in many ways to Fortran, and other languages were developed by research groups in Europe and the USA. Only a few of these have had any degree of success outside the environment in which they were produced, the main rival to Fortran being, perhaps, Algol 60. This is also a scientific language, aesthetically more satisfying to use than Fortran, but it did not have the driving force of a large computer manufacturer behind it at the time of its introduction, and so has tended to be used mainly in academic and research establishments. In the world of commerce, another high-level language known as COBOL (COmmon Business Oriented Language) became popular in the early 1960s and remains a firm favourite to the present day. In the mid-1960s, IBM introduced their System/360 range of computers, and with it a new language, PL/1—Programming Language Number One. This was intended to serve business and scientific interests equally, and is becoming very popular after rather a slow start.

In common with almost all other computer languages, Fortran is available in a number of dialects. The language has been subjected to a process of steady improvement, from the original Fortran through Fortran II, Fortran IV and now the American National Standards Institute's version, widely implemented, ANSI Fortran. So far as possible, this latter version is the one which will be dealt with in this book.

The compilation process

It has already been stated that the computer will only recognise and act upon instructions which are expressed in its own machine language. It was further pointed out that programs written in Fortran have to be translated, or compiled, into machine language.

A compiler is a *program* which is usually supplied with the computer system and is often stored permanently in the machine's memory. If the computer is a small one, the compiler may be supplied by the manufacturer in the form of a reel of punched paper tape, or as a deck of punched cards. These can usually be read in directly to the computer's memory, where they will be held in the form of machine language instructions. When this compiler program is activated, a program written in Fortran and punched into cards or tape can be loaded into the reader to be processed by the compiler. On small machines, the result of the compilation is that the computer punches out another card deck, or paper tape, containing the translated version of the program, in machine language. This may now be reloaded into the computer, which will execute the instructions presented to it. Fig. 1.2 gives a summary of the compilation process.

A procedure such as that outlined above is rather time-consuming. It involves the loading of at least three program decks (assuming that the primary input medium is punched cards) into the machine. When the Fortran program, or *source* program, has been loaded, it is necessary to wait while the machine language, or *object* program, is punched out. Larger and faster machines work on a slightly different system, though the essential features of the compiling system described above still apply. The system described next is intended to give rapid compilation and execution of the programs submitted, and is often known as the 'load-and-go' method.

Larger machines tend to have several types of memory,

some of which are faster in operation than others. The main store, where the instructions are held during execution, will usually be fastest and is often known as *core store*, because its basic component is the magnetic core.[1] Core store, however, is rather expensive and slower memory devices are used to supplement it. Among these may be magnetic tapes

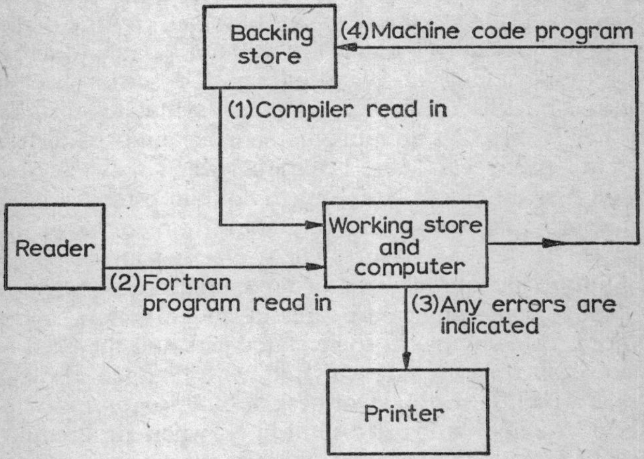

Fig. 1.2

and disks,[1] and it is on such devices as these that the larger computer is likely to keep copies of the compilers which are used. One of these will be the Fortran compiler. When the computer is told, by means of a suitable control instruction, that a Fortran program, or *job*, is ready for compilation, the compiler program is transferred from the magnetic tape or disk store into the faster core store of the machine.

The Fortran source program will be read into the machine, one card (containing one statement) at a time. The program may be processed immediately, or it may be stored on

[1] See *Electronic Computers* by F. L. Westwater (Teach Yourself Books).

magnetic tape or disk and dealt with later; whichever method is used, the basic principles are the same. As each Fortran statement is encountered, it is scanned carefully and checked for language errors. This check is quite automatic, and is performed by the computer acting under the direction of the Fortran compiler.

Fortran has its grammatical rules, just like any other language, and unless the rules are observed (by the person writing the program) the machine will not be able to understand the meaning of the program. The error-checking process is intended to find grammatical (syntactic) mistakes, and thus ensure that no ambiguous or meaningless instructions are produced. Most programs, when they are tried for the first time, will be found to contain errors, and the novice programmer should not allow himself to be discouraged by their occurrence. The two main sources of error are faulty punching of cards or tape, and lack of attention to apparently insignificant details in the grammar, such as the need for a comma in some statements and the need for its omission in others. It will frequently happen also that there is a fault in the logic, or design, of a program, but this will not usually be revealed until later, when an attempt is made to execute the program. The mere knowledge that an error exists is not very helpful, and most of the better compilers will try to pinpoint the source of the error. This may be by means of a simple numeric code or, in the more sophisticated systems, a detailed printed description of the error and its probable cause. If the meaning is obvious, some systems are able to undertake some limited remedial action and carry on as if nothing had happened, though a warning message may be printed. But when the error cannot be corrected, compilation of machine language will usually cease and only the error-checking scan will be performed. In this way, even though a program may not be compiled and executed, it will at least be examined thoroughly for *syntactic errors*.

Assuming that the program is free of such errors, as each statement is met, it is translated into the equivalent machine language. This newly translated program is retained within the computer's memory, either in core store or on one of the *backing store* devices (magnetic tape, for example). If it is in core store, it may be executed immediately. If not, it can be transferred into main memory for execution. The point of the system is that, once the Fortran program has been entered into the computer, no further intervention is required, other than to ensure that the data are so positioned as to be accessible to the program, before the results are produced.

Overall control

The reader may have wondered about the mechanism whereby the computer was able to activate the compiler program just at the moment it was needed, and how other seemingly automatic operations were performed. What has not been mentioned so far is that many computers will have in their memory another program whose function is supervisory and which controls the overall behaviour of the computer system, ensuring that the machine operations are nicely synchronised. This program is given different names by different manufacturers—Supervisor, Executive, Master Control Program have all been used and are more or less synonymous. Every aspect of the processing of programs fed into the computer, and the operation of its peripheral (i.e. auxiliary) devices, comes under the control of the Supervisor program. It also controls multi-programming on the larger machines. This is a technique whereby two or more independent programs can be held in the machine and, as far as the user is concerned, executed simultaneously. In this way, the usage of the facilities of the computer system can be optimised, and the wastage of valuable resources such as memory space can be kept to a minimum. This is important, since computers are very expensive to install and operate, and must be kept fully employed if their use is to be economically justifiable.

Two other terms which are sure to be encountered in the jargon-riddled world of the computer are *hardware* and *software*. Hardware is easy enough to define—think of the hard, physical parts of the computer, and these, lumped together, constitute its hardware. Software is more concerned with the programs which the computer system needs to fulfil its day-to-day commitments. Many of the functions of the computer are controlled by smaller auxiliary programs which are associated with the Supervisor. They may be used to perform certain arithmetic operations, or to control the peripheral devices, or to give the user necessary sorting facilities for his data, or to keep track of the passage of time, or any of a myriad of possibilities. This collection of useful programs, together with the compilers and the Supervisor, constitutes the software of the machine. One hears these days of 'hard software' (programs permanently wired into memory) and 'soft hardware' (easily changeable hardware features), but it is not the purpose of this book to discuss such developments. The important point is that the quality of the software supplied with a computer can make or mar the efficiency of the system as a whole.

Since Fortran programs have first to be translated into machine language, they take a rather longer time to process than the equivalent programs written in a language closer to machine language (machine language is rarely used these days, but there are languages known as *assembly languages* which are very close relatives to it, though very much easier to learn and write). Longer processing time means that more machine time is needed, which, in turn, implies a higher cost per program. This is offset, however, by the fact that programs are written very much more quickly in Fortran than they would be in assembly language, and they are usually more easily checked out. The compiler itself is very important here, as is the Supervisor program. If a compiler is slow, the cost is increased, but more efficient machine code may be produced. A fast compiler may not optimise the code produced to the same extent, and so the program produced may run quite slowly. Different circumstances call for different attacks on the problem, but a long program which is to be used frequently will usually need to be as fast in its operation as it is possible to make it. This economy may not be so important when a job is to be performed only once or twice. Many machines have two Fortran compilers, so that all-comers can be catered for.

Programming principles

The process of writing a program is fairly straightforward, but it does require that the problem under consideration is carefully analysed. The computer will do only those operations which it is instructed to perform—at least that is the case at this elementary level. Consequently, the instructions making up the program must be such that all possibilities are allowed for. For example, if the program does not contain a STOP instruction, it will carry on working until it is stopped by the intervention of the operator or the Supervisor program and is quite likely, as a result, to produce some unexpected results. By the time the reader has worked his way through this book he should be capable of writing a Fortran program and getting it to work.

Before any problem can be solved using a computer, the person who is to write the program must be very familiar with both the problem and the method to be used in solving it. This solution must be expressed as a sequence of simple steps which the machine can execute one after the other until the solution is achieved. This will usually mean the presentation of a series of algebraic formulae to the machine, together with the criteria needed for it to make certain logical decisions at key points of the calculation. The

Fortran system makes available a useful collection of 'library' programs which can be called upon to perform frequently required subcalculations, such as the extraction of square roots, logarithms, trigonometrical functions, and so on.

The analysis of the problem is very important, and when it has been done the actual writing of the program is almost a mechanical process. As in so many other fields, the process is clarified considerably when it is expressed in a pictorial form. The next chapter will be devoted to the pictorial development of an *algorithm*, which may be simply defined as a precise and concise specification of the method of solution of a problem.

2 Flowcharts

In the last chapter we saw that a computer will only respond to simple instructions. This implies that the solution to a problem will have to be expressed as a sequence of straightforward instructions which can be 'understood', and acted upon, by the computer. The high-level languages, such as Fortran, permit the use of instructions which are in many ways similar to the formulae of simple algebra. We can, for instance, cause the computer to add together two numbers by making use of the '+' sign, a feature unlikely to be found in a machine language.

Even though Fortran and similar high-level languages go a long way towards making programming easier, we still need to express the solution to the problem in an algebraic notation. One might truthfully say that no computer can solve a problem in its everyday applications—the real problem-solving is done by the programmer or analyst when he is preparing to write the program. The task of the computer is to relieve the tedium of numerical calculation.

Before we can write a Fortran program, therefore, we must be quite sure that we have understood the problem to be solved and that we have established in detail the sequence of operations to be performed in solving it—the so-called *logic* of the program. Unless the logic is correct, we cannot hope to produce a correctly working program, and it is here that the craft of the programmer lies. Fortunately, the craft is fairly easily acquired by most people interested in the subject.

Most people, at some time or other, must have prepared and used a shopping list. Why? Because such a list is useful as a memory aid, a help in planning a shopping trip. In many ways, such a list is rather like a rudimentary program—first call at the butcher, then put some petrol in the car, and so on. The sequence of events—the logic of the trip—is organised by the use of this device. In the same way that we are able to arrange and co-ordinate the logic of a shopping expedition by using a list, so we can make use of such an idea when we come to plan a program which is to be run on a computer.

We do not use a shopping list, of course; what we do use, often, is a *flowchart*. As its name implies, this is a technique whereby we can chart the sequence in which the operations constituting the program are performed—the flow of the program logic. It shows clearly the program's events and their interdependence.

All this is best illustrated by actually drawing a flowchart. Let us use the shopping trip mentioned above for our example. Suppose that we leave home by car, drive to the shops, then call at the butcher, the grocer and the hardware store, in that order. Having done this, we check the petrol in the car. If the level is low, then we should call at the garage to buy some. On the other hand, if there is enough left in the tank we shall drive straight home. Fig. 2.1 is a flowchart for this outing. Each of the boxes indicates a task to be performed, and these are joined by lines with arrows to show the order in which the tasks are to be executed. Note that the start point, the end point and what we may term the decision point are all clearly marked by distinctively shaped boxes.

We can make up a similar type of flowchart for all sorts of activities and processes. Such charts may contain portions in which the events follow sequentially, or there may be parts in which decisions are taken—whether to buy more petrol, for instance. A chart may be used to unravel complex, multi-way decisions. An example is given in Fig. 2.2, which deals with the process of letter-sorting in the Post Office. This is a fairly straightforward operation, but it involves the making of many decisions. The sorter must examine each letter and decide where, among the pigeon-holes which face him, it is to be placed. If you examine the

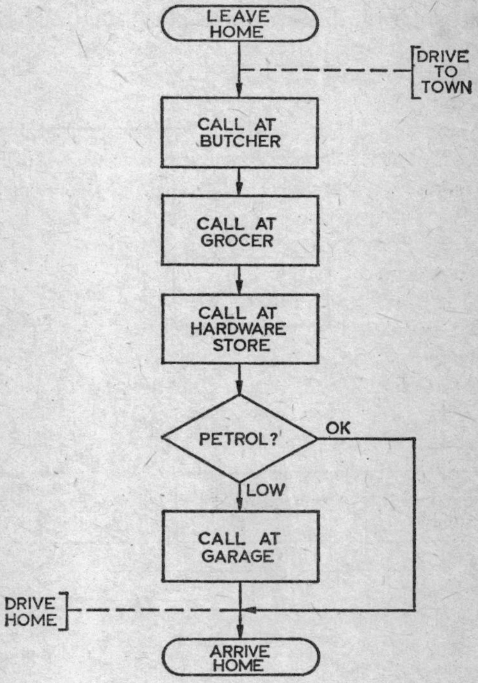

Fig. 2.1

chart carefully, following the arrows, you will see that the flow of logic forms a closed loop. After the man has picked up a letter, read the address and selected the appropriate pigeonhole, he then starts again at the top of the chart, picking up another letter, and so on. This idea of repeating a series of actions is a very important one—the computer's ability to perform such repetitions automatically is one of its main and most powerful features—and we shall meet it frequently. Notice that the arrows in the chart indicate the order in which the boxes are to be 'visited'. They will not

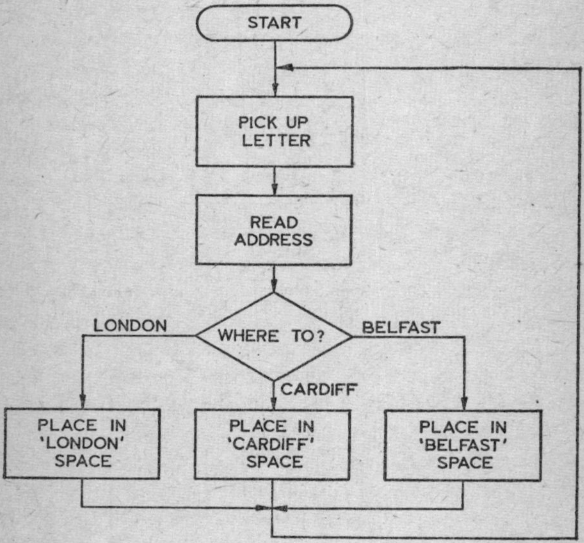

Fig. 2.2

always be given, the convention being that normal flow is from the top towards the bottom of a chart and from the left to the right side. Where the flow is not in accordance with the conventions, *or at any point where there might be ambiguity*, arrowheads should be added to the flowlines.

Now that we know what a flowchart looks like, let us consider a rather more complicated example—but again of a non-mathematical type.

John's date

John is a young man who is wondering whether or not to take his girlfriend, Mary, out for the evening. When John comes home, he must first decide whether he really wants to go out or not. If he doesn't, of course, there are no more problems to be solved except, perhaps, selection of a television programme. But let us assume that he does want to go out. The next problem, as with most young people, is whether he can afford it. Assuming that he can, all is well. If not—well, there's always Dad he can try to borrow from. Perhaps father has been asked once too often, in which case the problem of whether to take Mary out or not no longer exists.

John has the money. He knows that Mary will willingly walk into town provided that it is not raining. If it is raining, however, she will not want to go unless he has a car available. Two decisions are called for here: first, to determine whether or not it is raining and, if it is, to find out whether he can borrow the car. Finally, he has to discover whether Mary wants to go out or not.

So here we have a whole group of events and decisions which are dependent on one another. Why don't you try to draw a flowchart for the sequence, using the information given above? When you have finished, have a look at Fig. 2.3, which shows a suggested solution. The word 'suggested' is important, since there will usually be more than one way of drawing a flowchart for the solution of a particular problem. If your chart is not exactly the same as that given, therefore, it is not necessarily wrong. But do check it carefully to ensure that all the conditions implied in the problem are complied with. Two solutions may each lead to the right answer, but the programs produced may have different *efficiencies*—one may use less storage space or execution time than the other. Generally, as one gains in programming experience, one tends to write more efficient programs, or 'tighter code' as it is sometimes expressed.

Let us study Fig. 2.3 a little more closely, so that we completely understand what it is intended to represent.

John arrives home, as shown by the rounded 'terminal' box at the top of the flowchart. Flowcharts are usually drawn so that they may be read from top to bottom. This rule is not invariable, but such an arrangement does make the chart easier to follow (in the Western world) and this type of layout should be adopted whenever possible. Incidentally, it is worth making the effort to ensure that flowlines do not cross one another except on very rare occasions—this also avoids possible confusion. On very complicated charts, of course, these rules may be relaxed a little.

Following the flow as indicated by the arrows, we reach a 'decision box', at which John decides whether he wants to take Mary out or not. An answer of 'no' will, so far as this example is concerned, mean that he will stay home, and so the line corresponding to the 'no' decision leads immediately to the event box STAY HOME at the bottom of the chart. We would say, more formally, that the answer 'no' initiates a *branch* to the STAY HOME event. If John decides to take Mary out, then we follow the line labelled 'yes' to the next box in the main sequence. This is another decision box which determines whether or not he can afford to go out. The answer to this question generates a branch to other events or decisions, and so on throughout the chart. Usually, a decision box will have only two exits—'yes' and 'no', 'true' and 'false', 'equal' and 'not equal', etc.—but the sorting office example gives an instance of the not infrequent case of the multiple decision. The point made earlier about there being more than one correct solution can be appreciated better now, perhaps, in conjunction with the study of Fig. 2.3. We could, for instance, have assumed that John would have considered the possibility of its raining and of his having to borrow a car before any idea of being able to afford

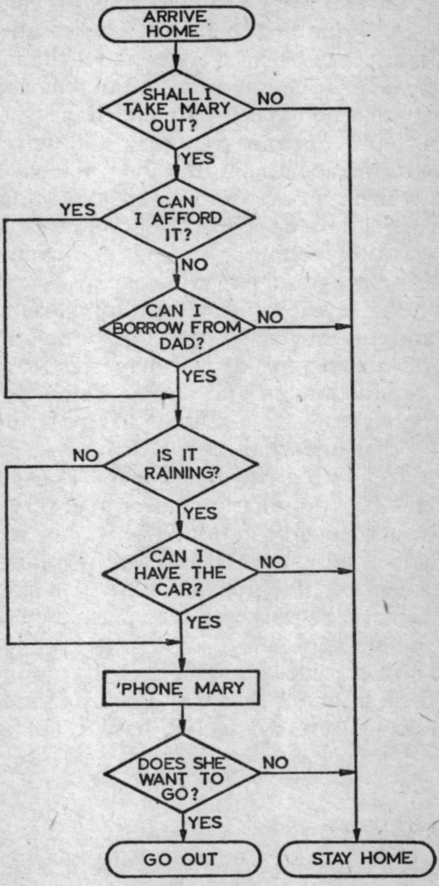
ARRIVE HOME
SHALL I TAKE MARY OUT?
NO
YES
CAN I AFFORD IT?
YES
NO
CAN I BORROW FROM DAD?
NO
YES
IS IT RAINING?
NO
YES
CAN I HAVE THE CAR?
NO
YES
'PHONE MARY
DOES SHE WANT TO GO?
NO
YES
GO OUT
STAY HOME

Fig. 2.3

the trip and borrow from his father entered his head. Just for practice, try redrawing Fig. 2.3 using this changed order of events—i.e. John first considers the weather and its possible consequences, then worries about the money.

Problems such as these may seem far removed from the programming of a digital computer. Well, yes, in a way this is true, for most Fortran programs will have a certain amount of arithmetic in them. But the principle of reducing a complex sequence of events and decisions into an ordered grouping using a device such as the flowchart to keep track of the logic is of general application, and cannot be overemphasised. As programmers grow in experience, they may tend to become less dependent on flowcharts for simpler problems, and this may be all right for a 'one-off' job which has to be got working quickly and may never be used again. But for a production program—one which may be used regularly for years—it is essential that it be documented carefully, so that any changes which may be needed (for instance, to deal with a new tax, like VAT) can be quickly incorporated. The flowchart will form a very important part of any such documentation. The way in which a program works is usually far better shown by a flowchart than by the statements of the program itself. The mass of detail contained in most programs tends to mask the basic process of solving the problem.

We shall now consider some more problems and the flowcharts for their solutions, but this time using examples of a more numerical nature. Let us first have a look at a mathematical example.

The Fibonacci series

This is simply a sequence of numbers in which each member of the series is derived from the values of the two numbers which immediately precede it in the sequence. In fact, the value of each term is the sum of the two numbers which precede it in the series. It follows that once we have defined the values of the first two terms in the series we can calculate the values of as many other terms as we wish. For example, suppose that the first two terms each have the value 1. That is to say, the series starts off looking like this:

1 1 . . .

What will be the value of the third, fourth and subsequent terms? Bearing in mind the way in which the series is defined, namely that each term is the sum of the two preceding terms, the third term must be equal in value to the second term added to the first term. That is to say, $1 + 1 = 2$. We now have:

1 1 2 . . .

The fourth term will be the sum of the third and second terms, giving:

1 1 2 3 . . .

and so on, and the first ten terms will be:

1 1 2 3 5 8 13 21 34 55 . . .

Now suppose that a program must be written to compute the values of the terms of such a series, given the first two terms, and that 100 such values are to be calculated. Although the detailed preparation of the program is at present beyond us, we can at least draw up a flowchart representing the *algorithm* (method of solution) to be used.

Where do we start? Well, the first two terms may both have the value 1, but this is not necessarily so, and we should allow for their being changed by the user of the program. So perhaps we should arrange that the values of these terms are read at the beginning of the program.

We can make a list showing the sequence of events which must occur:

1. Read in the values of the first and second terms, and print them.
2. Add these together to form the third term and print this.
3. Add the second and third terms to form the fourth term and print it.
4. Add the third and fourth terms to form the fifth term and print it.
5. Add the fourth and fifth terms . . ., etc.

Rather than write a new section of program for the calculation of each successive term, we may use the idea of a *loop*, or repeated execution of a sequence of instructions. A glance at Fig. 2.4 will reveal one way in which this problem might be approached. Each term of the series is denoted by the letter a to which a *subscript* has been attached. For example, a_1 is the first term, a_{29} is the twenty-ninth term, and so on. Each term will have a numerical value, of course, but it is convenient to use symbols such as a to define a general solution. If you look at Fig. 2.4 you will see, after the START box at the head of the chart, that the first two actions involve the reading of values for the first two terms, a_1 and a_2. The expression 'to read' is often used to mean that the computer obtains items of data supplied by the user, usually from punched cards or punched paper tape. The details of this *input* process, and the corresponding process for *output* of results, will be dealt with later in the book.

The next box introduces another symbol, i, which will be used as a *counter* so that we shall know when the appropriate number of terms has been computed. Such symbols which are used to name values that can vary during the execution of the program are called *variables*. At this stage of the process, a value of 3 is to be given the variable i.

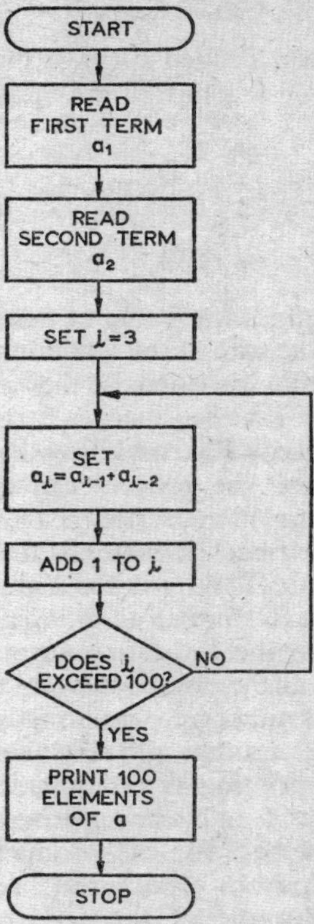
START
READ FIRST TERM a1
READ SECOND TERM a2
SET i=3
SET ai=ai-1+ai-2
ADD 1 TO i
DOES i EXCEED 100?
NO
YES
PRINT 100 ELEMENTS OF a
STOP

Fig. 2.4

The next box specifies that a formula is to be used:

$$a_i = a_{i-1} + a_{i-2}$$

Since i has just been defined to have the value 3, we can interpret the formula has having the meaning

$$a_3 = a_{3-1} + a_{3-2}$$

or, after some elementary arithmetic on the subscripts,

$$a_3 = a_2 + a_1$$

This, of course, defines the value of the third term of our Fibonacci series—the sum of the two immediately preceding terms. The next action is to increase the value of the variable i, and following that a check is made on its value. If the increased value exceeds 100, we know that 100 values have been calculated, and the process can continue with the printing of the terms of the series. If the new value of i is 100 or less, a branch back is made to the point at which a new term is calculated. (Why is the test on i to determine whether it *exceeds* 100 rather than whether it is *equal to* 100?) Finally, when the 100 terms have been printed, the process terminates at the box containing the word STOP.

This process does not correspond exactly to the numbered scheme given earlier, in that all the values have been computed before any printing is attempted. This avoids the special case of terms 1 and 2 being printed separately. Fig. 2.5 is another flowchart for the production of the same series, but is much more economical because it does not have to store the whole of the series before output is initiated. At each stage, only the two terms needed for the calculation of the next term are retained, and those not needed are discarded after the output. Note the necessity for output within the loop in this case, and the special process needed for terms 1 and 2. The reader will find a careful study of this example quite rewarding.

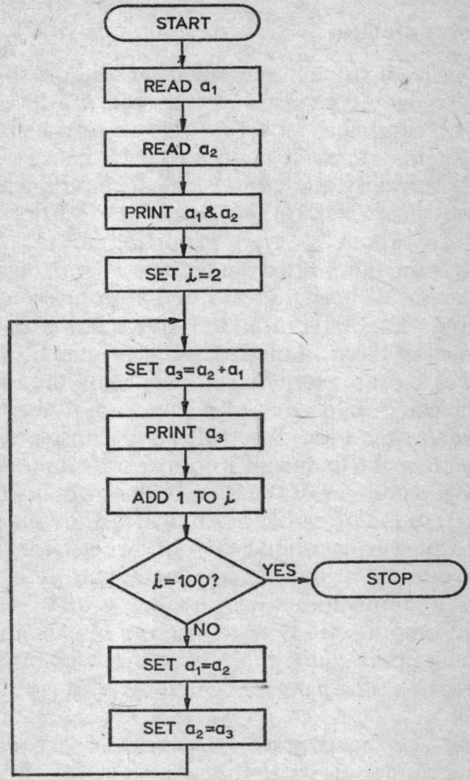
START
READ a_1
READ a_2
PRINT a_1 & a_2
SET $i=2$
SET $a_3=a_2+a_1$
PRINT a_3
ADD 1 TO i
$i=100$?
YES
STOP
NO
SET $a_1=a_2$
SET $a_2=a_3$

Fig. 2.5

Now here is a somewhat different example.

A conversion problem

Imagine yourself to be a manufacturer and distributor of a very wide range of goods, and that you produce for your customers a catalogue—a very extensive one, listing several thousand items. A major feature of each item is its height, and this is currently quoted in yards, feet and inches. Trade connections have been established with the EEC countries, and you are about to start exporting to the European continent from the United Kingdom. It will obviously be in the interests of both yourself and your customers if you can produce a new edition of your catalogue in which dimensions are given in metres and centimetres. The problem is, then, to draw a flowchart showing how the appropriate conversion can be carried out for each item in the catalogue.

Once again, the procedure will be to consider each item in turn, to convert its height into metric form and to print the catalogue number of the item followed by its converted height. Before looking at Fig. 2.6, which shows a suggested solution, have a go at producing your own version, assuming that there are 2000 items in the catalogue. It is probable that your solution will not be the same as that given in Fig. 2.6, but you should still be sure that you understand all that is happening in that diagram. Notice that a counter is again being used, this time *purely* as a counter and with the name N.

First we set the counter, N, equal to zero—we have nothing to count yet, since the process is just beginning—and then enter the main loop. Here, each time round the loop, we read the reference number of the next item to be dealt with and the height of the item in yards (Y), feet (F) and inches (I). This having been done, the height is converted to its equivalent in inches and then multiplied by the conversion factor, 0.0254, to give a result in metres and

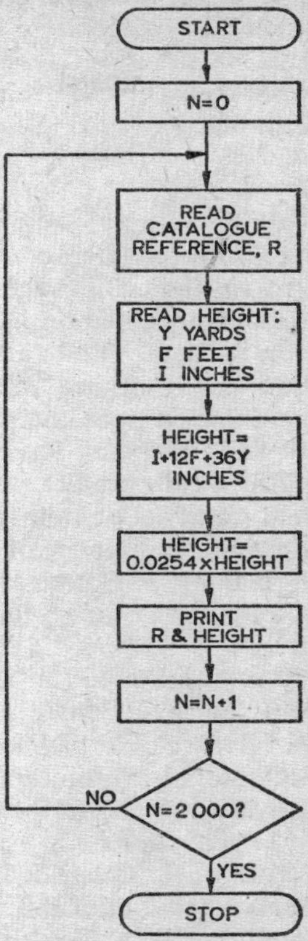
START
N=0
READ CATALOGUE REFERENCE, R
READ HEIGHT:
Y YARDS
F FEET
I INCHES
HEIGHT=
I+12F+36Y
INCHES
HEIGHT=
0.0254xHEIGHT
PRINT
R & HEIGHT
N=N+1
N=2 000?
NO
YES
STOP

Fig. 2.6

fractions of a metre. The reference number of the item and its converted height value are then printed, and one is added to the count. The count is then checked to see if it has reached the final value, here 2000, and if it has the process is terminated. Otherwise, a backward branch is performed to read the details of the next item.

A payroll calculation

As the final example of this chapter, consider the case of a program designed to calculate the wages of workers in a factory. This is quite a complicated problem in practice, for there are many factors to be taken into account: income tax at varying rates, National Insurance, merit awards, bonus schemes, and so on, all increase the complexity of the arithmetic and the logic of the program. Basically, however, the problem is a straightforward one. Let us consider the case of the employees paid weekly at an hourly rate: the calculation involves multiplying the number of hours worked by the rate per hour, making any necessary deductions or additions occasioned by, for instance, income tax or overtime working.

Suppose that a firm employs 400 men in this category. Each man works a 40-hour week, anything above this being classified as overtime. The rate for payment is, say, P pence per hour, and the additional overtime rate is X pence per hour. (Note that this is *additional to* the P pence per hour already being paid.) Deductions for National Insurance amount to N pence per week. Other deductions total one-tenth of what remains after National Insurance has been taken out. You should now be able to draw a flowchart to calculate the wage of each employee in a given week. Do so, and compare your answer with the solution suggested in Fig. 2.7. Here, HOURS is the total time worked by each man during the week, WAGE is the final resulting payment after all deductions have been made. DEDS is the sum of

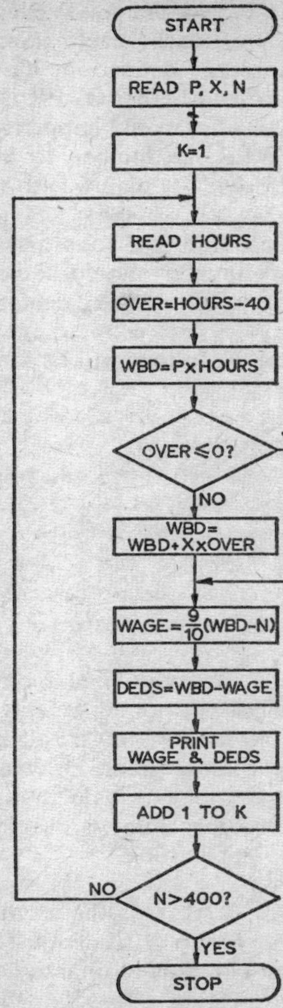
START
READ P, X, N
K=1
READ HOURS
OVER=HOURS-40
WBD=PxHOURS
OVER≤0?
YES
NO
WBD=
WBD+XxOVER
WAGE=9/10(WBD-N)
DEDS=WBD-WAGE
PRINT
WAGE & DEDS
ADD 1 TO K
NO
N>400?
YES
STOP

Fig. 2.7

the deductions made in each case and OVER is the number of hours of overtime worked by each man. In addition, WBD is the wage before any deductions have been made. Why is a check made to see whether OVER is negative? To answer this question, see what would happen if the test were not performed and OVER *did* happen to be negative—a situation which would occur if a man was to work less than 40 hours in the week.

Again, you are likely to find that your answer varies from that given. No further comment should be necessary, however, for you to be able to follow the calculations.

Before continuing to the next chapter, try the following exercises in flowcharting. Solutions will be found at the end of the book.

Exercises

1. Draw the flowchart of a process to add together the first fifty numbers (i.e. 1 + 2 + 3 + 4 + . . . etc.) and print the result.

2. Construct a flowchart for the process of converting a length expressed in inches into yards, feet and inches.

3. A manufacturer sells chemicals, and his catalogue lists them at so many pence per pound weight. He wishes to sell in France, and so has to convert all his prices into French new francs per kilogramme. Draw a flowchart for the process of conversion. (Assume that there are 2.2 pounds (weight) to a kilogramme, and that there are 12 new francs to the pound sterling.)

4. A program is required to classify the results of examinations taken by a large group of students. There are to be four classes: the first contains all marks less than 45%; the next covers the range 46% to 55%; the third group contains results all of which lie between 56% and 65%;

and the last group contains all marks of 66% and higher. It is required to know the number of results in each group. Assume that the results of 10 000 candidates are to be classified. The program should print out four numbers: the first will be the number of results in group 1, the second will be the number of results in group 2, and so on. Draw a flowchart for this program.

5. A bus company needs to analyse the fuel consumption of its fleet of buses. For each vehicle, results are obtainable which show the number of miles driven and the amount of fuel used during a test period. The number of buses in the fleet is B. Draw a flowchart to show the calculation of the average fuel consumption of a bus in miles per gallon, for the fleet as a whole.

6. In a certain year, the income tax paid by a married man without children was calculated as follows:

   Two-ninths of the total income plus a further sum of £240.00 was free of tax. The remainder of the income, called the *taxable income*, was charged in accordance with the following rules.

   The first £50.00 was charged at 11p in the pound. The rate on the next £150.00 was 34p, and on any further taxable income the rate was 43p in the pound.

   Draw a flowchart for a program to calculate the tax payable by a set of such men, each having a different gross income. Suppose that the group considered contains 500 men.

3 Constants and variables

In this chapter we shall examine some of the basic ideas and principles upon which the Fortran language is based. Some of these concepts will seem rather strange at first, and the rules may appear unduly restrictive, even unnecessary. Rules are important in any language, however, and Fortran is no exception: all the rules given to you in this and the remaining chapters of the book must be carefully observed every time you write a program.

Did you understand what is implied by the paragraph above. Whether you answer 'yes' or 'no', you have obviously understood the question. But, if you were a computer, the chances are that you would not have been able to understand, since the sentence contains an error of syntax—it has no question mark at the end. Your imagination and experience will have enabled you to supply the missing piece of syntactic information yourself, but a computer in normal circumstances would be unable to do so. In consequence, it would either have indicated that it was not able to understand or perhaps have gone on blindly and produced the wrong answers. And let there be no illusions here: if a computer is presented with meaningless or erroneous data, it will produce equally meaningless results—the computer is not, contrary to popular opinion, infallible. Both the program and the data supplied must be free of errors before the answers may be considered reliable. The digital computer has no implicit intelligence. All that it can do is to obey instructions, and that only when those instructions are presented in a very precise form. It will never guess: when there is uncertainty it will stop and rely on human intervention to put things right. Why, then, do we use such ignorant beasts? The answer lies in the fact that the very precision with which they follow orders, and the speed with which they do arithmetic, makes them far superior to the human mind for performing routine calculating tasks where speed and accuracy are of prime importance. Accuracy when programming is thus essential. You are learning a language —Fortran—but you must be far more careful to obey all the rules than you would if you were learning a natural language such as French or Italian. Luckily, there are not too many of these rules, and they are fairly easily learnt. These remarks apply throughout the rest of this book, but especially to the remainder of this chapter.

The idea of a constant

One thing that every British schoolboy learns to do is to convert pounds to pence. Let us consider the way it is done. Suppose that we have £A and wish to calculate the equivalent number of pence. There are no prizes for knowing the formula:

number of pence = A * 100

Note the use of the symbol * to indicate multiplication. It will be used throughout the book.

If we had £V instead of £A, the conversion factor would still have been 100, since there are 100 pence in one pound sterling. The value '100' can thus be regarded as a *constant*— it always has the same value. There are always 100 pence in one pound.

Any number is a constant. Another example is 747. Constants may be fractional: the circumference of a circle is given by the formula

circumference = 2 * pi * radius

in which ‘pi’ is the name of a constant having the approximate value 3.14159. 2, of course, is a whole-number constant.

Incidentally, there is a basic difference between these two numbers: pi contains a decimal point, whereas 2 does not. When we do arithmetic in everyday life, we usually take decimal points very much for granted. It does not normally matter very much whether we express a constant as ‘20’ or as ‘20.0’, or even as ‘20.’, for if a decimal point is omitted from a whole number we still understand what is intended, and in practice all three representations mean the same thing. To a computer using Fortran, however, there is a very important difference between ‘20’ and ‘20.0’, though both are constants. The form without the decimal point has some specialised and important uses, whereas much of our arithmetic is likely to involve numbers which contain an explicit decimal point. In what follows, constants which do *not* contain a decimal point will be referred to as INTEGER constants, while those which *do* contain a decimal point will be called REAL constants. These are also called, occasionally, *fixed-point* and *floating-point* constants respectively. These names are derived from the way in which the computer organises its arithmetic: floating-point arithmetic is a method of number manipulation used by computers to ease the problem of keeping track of the decimal point in involved arithmetic processes and requires that the numbers be represented in a special form, whereas fixed-point numbers have a straightforward representation and the decimal point is assumed to be in the same place—often at the end of the number—throughout any arithmetic processing which may occur.

Floating-point arithmetic is of great importance, and it may be worth while our giving it a little more detailed study. The first thing which should be realised is that the size of numbers which can be represented inside a computer is limited, since there is a physical limit on the length of the registers in which the numbers are held whilst they are being processed. We shall not concern ourselves with the details of this processing here: the interested reader is referred to one of the many descriptive texts available, of which the companion book to this (*Electronic Computers* by F. L. Westwater) is one of the cheapest.

This limitation on the size of numbers leads to immediate difficulties. Consider the case of a computer whose *word-length* (the normal maximum number of digits in a register) is eight decimal digits, which is to be used to multiply together the numbers 210 000 and 120 000. We can work the result out by hand, and find that:

$$210\,000 * 120\,000 = 25\,200\,000\,000$$

This is rather awkward, since the result contains eleven digits and our machine's registers can only hold eight. What can we do about this? Well, one approach is to represent the numbers in a different way.

210 000, for instance, could be rewritten as 21.0 * 10000, or $21.0 * 10^4$ (i.e. 21.0 multiplied by the fourth power of 10). Another way of writing the same number would be as $0.21 * 10^6$. There are, as you will realise, many other ways of representing the value. It is found, however, that the maximum precision can be maintained during the arithmetic processes if the *mantissa* (the part of the number which is to be multiplied by a power of 10) is a fraction between 0 and 1. The power of 10 by which multiplication is effected is called the *exponent*, and mantissa and exponent together constitute a floating-point number.

In the Fortran language, the number $0.21 * 10^6$ would be written as 0.21E6, where 'E' represents '* 10' and the exponent, 6, is written *on* the line rather than above it, since the equipment used in the preparation of a program for input to the computer usually has no means of representing superscripts or, for that matter, subscripts. This problem has to be overcome by the use of special symbols, and 'E' is one of these.

Now try writing the other number, 120 000, in this new way, without looking at the answer given below.

Did you get it right? 120 000 = $0.12 * 10^6$, which translates into the Fortran number 0.12E6. If you had the simpler version .12E6, this would be equally valid, as would 1.2E5, or any of the many possible combinations.

When using Fortran, you may represent numbers in their familiar decimal form (but don't forget the decimal point), or you may use this new form. Both ways are quite acceptable. The exponential (E) form is perhaps best reserved for very large and very small numbers.

Numbers tend to be rather more complicated than the simple examples which have been quoted so far. One has to deal with negative values and small fractions. Thus, either or both the mantissa and the exponent of a floating-point number may be negative, which will be indicated by preceding it by a minus sign (—). Also, if it is felt that its use will clarify the meaning, positive values may be identified by preceding them by a plus sign (+). But if a plus sign is not given, it will be understood to be there unless a minus sign explicitly appears.

For example, suppose it is required to express —2970.0 in floating-point form:

—2970.0 = —.297E+4

The first minus sign indicates that the number as a whole is negative, and the plus sign in the middle of the number shows that the mantissa is to be raised to a positive power of 10. But, in practice, the plus sign would normally be omitted, thus: —.297E4

Either sign may be omitted if it is plus, but not if it is minus.

Here is another example: express 0.0316 in exponential form.

0.0316 = +.316E−1

This means that 10 has to be raised to a negative power—the exponent is negative. In other words, we are to *divide* by a power of 10 rather than to multiply by it. A list of numbers and the corresponding exponential forms is given below. Check each example carefully and the principles of floating-point representation should soon become clear. Further exercises are provided at the end of the chapter for practice.

916.8 = +.9168E3
−.9168 = −.9168E0
−.009168 = −.9168E−2
9168.0 = +.9168E4

Generally, we shall use the more familiar number representations, but the exponential form is useful when dealing with very large or very small numbers: .562E21 is a lot easier to write than

562000000000000000000.0

and similarly .2365E−15 is much easier to write, *and less error prone*, than

0.0000000000000002365

Returning to the example of multiplication with which we started, we now see that the expression

210 000.0 * 120 000.0

must be replaced by

.21E6 * .12E6

and, if you think back to your schooldays when you dealt with indices, you will see that this is equivalent to the expression

(.21 * .12)E(6+6)
i.e. .0252E12
or .252E11

Translating back to 'ordinary' numbers, this will be seen to be the same as 25 200 000 000.0—the answer we expect, but expressed with far fewer characters.

Floating-point numbers can represent very large numbers indeed (and very small ones, too, of course). For example, 0.99E99 represents the number 99 followed by 97 zeros—an enormous number. But the computer registers are still limited in size, and this will cause limitations on the number of significant figures which may be held in the floating-point mantissa. So this system does not necessarily give greater accuracy to our calculations and must be used with care and understanding, but the problems of keeping track of the decimal point are automated, thus simplifying the task of the programmer. For the examples given in this book, the errors which the use of floating-point arithmetic may introduce are insignificant, but the user should know that such errors can arise. A treatment of the topic is outside the scope of this book.

Having dealt with constants, which have a fixed value throughout the execution of a program, let us consider the *variable*, which doesn't!

Variables

We have already briefly met this term in the previous chapter. Now the idea will be examined more closely, with particular emphasis on the part played by variables in the Fortran language.

Earlier in this chapter we looked at the way in which pounds can be converted into pence. To effect this conversion, we multiplied the number of pounds, A, by a constant which, in this case, was 100. It was pointed out at the time that if we had £V and not £A the method would remain unchanged. The numerical value which we could assign to A or V did not enter into the argument—we might have been considering £5 or £20 000. The value of A is completely variable, and A itself is referred to as a Fortran *variable.*

Names of variables need not be restricted to single letters. We could rewrite our conversion formula as:

PENCE = POUNDS * 100.0

where PENCE and POUNDS are both names of variables. You will recall that variable names were used in Chapter 2, to simplify the contents of flowchart boxes.

As might be expected, there are one or two rules which must be observed when making up variable names, and these are given below. Read them carefully—many Fortran errors are the result of not following them!

1. The name of a variable *must* begin with an alphabetic character. Only capital letters may be used, but all the letters from A to Z are available.
2. The number of characters in a variable name must not exceed six.
3. After the first character, subsequent characters may, if you wish, be digits. Any of the decimal digits 0 to 9 may be used. There is no obligation to use digits, however; the choice is yours.
4. Some sequences of letters and digits have a special meaning in Fortran and should not, in general, be used as variable names. Examples are SIN and COS. We shall meet these again later.
5. Special characters, such as '+' or '—', may not be used in variable names—letters and digits only, please.

The following are examples of valid variable names:

A	ALPHA	Q294GH	POUNDS	APPLES	D9
RMS	DATA1	H71922	ZZZZ	T	FRED

It should be noted that, although the maximum length of a variable name has been given as six characters, some computer systems may permit names longer than this or specify that they should contain fewer characters. The standard length, however, is six characters, and this is the value which will be used in this book. If you are able to use a computer to check your programs, check with the Fortran manual for your particular machine in case there is any local variation in the rules.

Just as there are real and integer constants, so there are real and integer variables. An *integer* variable is one which can take only whole-number values (no decimal point), such as 20 or 20978: it cannot take values such as 29.879 or 3.142, which are *real* values and may be contained only in real variables. The next problem is to distinguish between real and integer variables. This is very important, since mixed arithmetic between real and integer values is not, in general, permitted.

Integer variables begin with one of the letters I, J, K, L, M or N.

The following are examples of integer variable names:

ITEM   I3012   K   J7   MAVIS   N4N5N6

Variable names which begin with any other letter are of real type.

Let us review what has been said about variables so far.

Variables may be of two main types: real and integer. Integer variable names begin with one of the letters I, J, K, L, M or N. Variable names should not normally contain more than six characters, of which the first must be alphabetic and the remainder must be *alphanumeric* (either alphabetic or numeric). Special characters are not permitted. Integer variables can contain only whole-number values. Real variables will contain floating-point values.

To emphasise what a variable name should *not* look like, study the following examples of *incorrect* variable names. The reasons for their invalidity are given alongside each example.

COMPUTER	—more than six characters;
1ABLE	—first character is not alphabetic;
AC+192	—contains a special character (+);
SIN	—this may be regarded by many Fortran systems as a reserved word, having a special interpretation which will be dealt with later in the book. Although not strictly incorrect as a variable name it should be avoided.

The exercises at the end of this chapter will give further practice in forming and interpreting variable names. Now let us consider some other applications of the variable.

Subscripted variables

Suppose that we have the job of analysing a set of figures relating to a stock control problem. This might involve our carrying out a relatively simple calculation on a large amount of data relating to all the items which make up the stock. There might be thousands of these items, and it would be most inconvenient if, assuming certain items of data to be variable in nature—stock level, delivery period, for example —we had to assign a unique variable name to each item. We might refer to the stock level of item 1 as STOCK1, to that of item 2 as STOCK2, and so on, inventing a different name for each item. Since the same type of calculation would probably be needed for each item, the flowchart for a program might appear, in part, like Fig. 3.1 overleaf.

This is very unsatisfactory. Why bother with a computer at all? The instructions have to be repeated for every item. It would be better, surely, to supply instructions to the computer once only and have them applied to each item. Look back to the work we did in Chapter 2, and the answer will be apparent—a loop will be used. And the *subscripted* variable will help achieve our aim.

What we might consider doing is to use only *one* variable name for the stock levels of *all* the items in the list. Suppose we do this and adopt the name STOCK. On the face of it, this does not help much—there are still thousands of items, but only one name—aren't we back where we started?

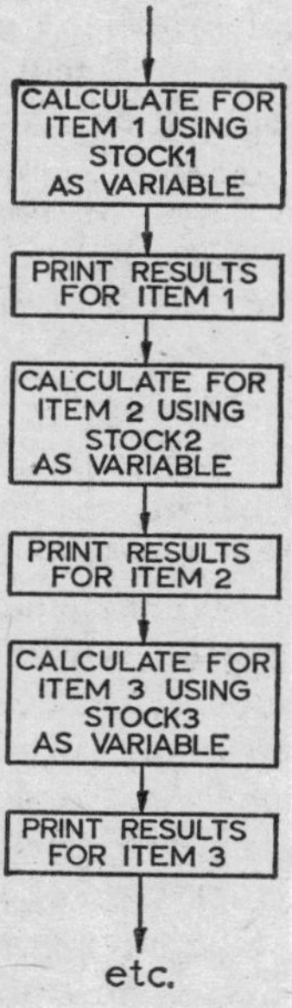

Fig. 3.1

No, not quite. We can *subscript* the variable name to distinguish between the various items: item 1 can be referred to as $STOCK_1$, item 2 may be called $STOCK_2$, and so on. Well, you may say, there does not appear to be very much difference between the names STOCK1, STOCK2, and $STOCK_1$, $STOCK_2$. In fact, there is: STOCK1 and STOCK2 are two entirely different Fortran variables, but $STOCK_1$

and $STOCK_2$ are simply different 'facets' of the same variable STOCK—more precisely, they are two separate *elements* of the *array* STOCK, distinguished by the subscripts 1 and 2. Notice that STOCK is the name of a real variable, so that *all* the elements of the array will be of real type. One may, of course, have arrays of integer values: you might care to consider what form their names would take. To review: an array is a set of items which may be referred to by one name, whose individual elements can be distinguished by appending subscripts to that name.

It is not possible to punch subscripts in their form as shown above when preparing a program for input to a computer. In fact, it is necessary to write, for instance, $STOCK_1$ as STOCK(1), with the subscript in parentheses following the variable name.

The parentheses are very important, and must not be omitted. This does not, as you might think, break the rule about special characters not being allowed in variable names: the name here is STOCK, and (1) is the subscript held in parentheses. STOCK(1) is a *subscripted variable.*

The subscript must *always* be of *integer* type. We shall see that the subscript may take the form of a constant, variable or simple arithmetic expression.

For example, we could write STOCK(J), and the particular element of the array STOCK to which we were referring would be dependent on the current value of the integer variable J. If J has the value 1, we should be considering the element $STOCK_1$. We could make the value of J equal to 29, in which case we would be dealing with the 29th element, $STOCK_{29}$, and so on. Instead of having to rename the variables when we refer to a different item, and write the instructions again, all that is now needed is to arrange to change the value of J after each calculation and then use the same instructions over again. Fig. 3.2 is part of a flowchart for the same problem, using this principle.

The subscripting facility is one of the most useful features of high-level languages such as Fortran. But it has broader applications than those which have been discussed so far.

Up until now we have considered only the 'one-dimensional' array—that is, there has been only one subscript in

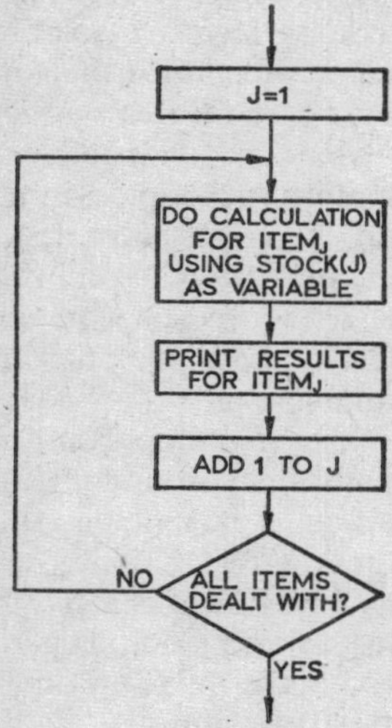

Fig. 3.2

the parentheses following the variable name. The Fortran language does not restrict our use of subscripts to the one-dimensional case, and two or three subscripts may be used when necessary. In practice, however, there are often restrictions imposed by the Fortran compiler being used, and these will vary from computer to computer.

What are the circumstances in which one would want to use more than one subscript? Here is an example which may clarify the situation.

Consider a grid such as that used for playing the game of noughts and crosses (or tic-tac-toe). It has nine squares arranged in a square formation, as shown in Fig. 3.3, in which the columns and rows have been numbered from 1 to 3. Suppose that each of the small squares contains a number, and it is required to find the number contained in the square marked X. Let us further suppose that the

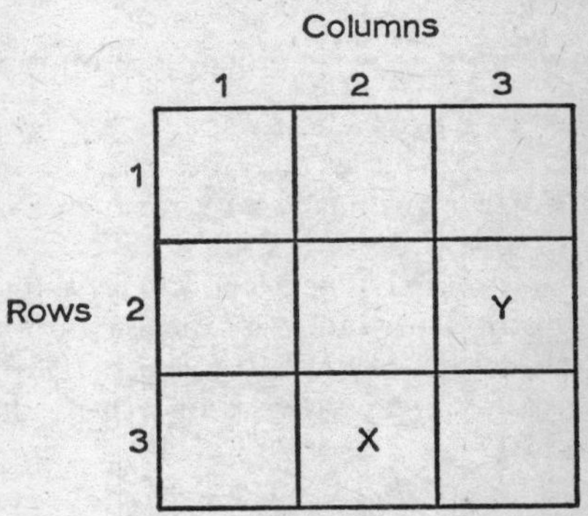

Fig. 3.3

numbers are elements of an array called DATA. If DATA is a one-dimensional array, then the number in the square marked X might be referenced by the subscripted variable DATA(8) if the information were held in DATA in rows, or by DATA(6) if the information were stored by columns. It is not easy to see from the diagram exactly which element of data corresponds to the square with X in it.

By making use of the numbers associated with each row and column, it is possible to be quite precise as to which array element is used. The square marked X is in row 3, column 2. We may abbreviate this to a pair of subscripts (3,2)—the first subscript, by convention, always specifying the row and the second indicating the column. We then declare that DATA is a two-dimensional array and refer to the square marked X as DATA(3,2): X marks the square at the intersection of the third row and second column of the array called DATA. What would you need to write to refer to the element marked Y in Fig. 3.3?

Yes, Y marks the element DATA(2,3). Note the comma which separates the subscripts *and must never be omitted.*

In summary, the format of a two-dimensional subscripted variable is

variable name(row number, column number)

It is permitted to leave as many spaces between the variable name and its subscripts as may be desired. In fact, spaces are used in Fortran primarily as a means of improving the readability of the program and, with one exception, are ignored by the compiler. The exception is easily remembered, and will be dealt with later. In the meantime, use spaces wherever you feel they ought to appear. It follows that the following are all equivalent ways of writing the subscripted variable DATA(1,2):

```
DATA(1,2)  DATA (1,2)  DATA (1, 2)  DATA ( 1 , 2 )
  D A T A ( 1 , 2 )
```

Again, the subscripts must be integer constants, variables or expressions.

Just to ensure that the ideas of two-dimensional arrays have been thoroughly understood, look for a moment at Fig. 3.4. Here we have returned to the problem of stock control. For each item there will be certain information such as stock level, buffer stock, price, etc. If we specify that all the information in the table shown is to be considered as contained in a two-dimensional array TABLE, then it is apparent that for item number 2:

TABLE(2,4) is the delivery time
TABLE(2,2) is the buffer stock

What, in the same terms, is the weekly demand for item number 4? The answer is TABLE(4,5). There are more exercises for you at the end of the chapter.

Item	Stock level	Buffer stock	Price	Delivery time	Weekly demand
1					
2					
3					
4					
5					

Fig. 3.4

Three-dimensional arrays are an extension of what we have dealt with so far. Each element of such an array will have three subscripts: an example would be PLACE(I,J,K). It may help, if the idea is unfamiliar, to think of a three-dimensional array as a pile of two-dimensional arrays: the first subscript selects one of these subarrays and the second and third 'home-in' on the specific element required.

Some of the smaller computers will not allow the use of more than two subscripts. Again, you should consult the Fortran manual of the installation for which you expect to write programs.

Further notes about subscripts

Until now, we have only considered array elements of the form A(I), in which the subscript or subscripts are single integer constants or variables. Fortran permits us a little more flexibility than this, however, for we may use simple arithmetic expressions as subscripts. Consider this example:

A(I+3)

If I has the value 5, then we are referring to the (5+3)rd element of the array A, in other words A(8).

As always, we must stick to the rules.

1. The subscript expression must involve only integer quantities—variables and constants. A(I—2) is permissible, but A(I—2.0) is not.
2. The value of the subscript must always work out as a whole number *greater than zero.* In the example of rule 1 above, it is important that the value of I is never allowed to become less than 3. If it did, the subscript expression would have a value of zero or less, and the result of such an occurrence is, in general, unpredictable.
3. Only a restricted range of arithmetic expressions is allowed inside the subscript parentheses. These are fully defined below, where J represents an integer variable, k and kk represent integer constants.

Subscript expression	**Typical example**
J	LIST(I)
k	LIST(4)
J+k	LIST(I+4)
J—k	LIST(I—4)
k*J	LIST(4*I)
k*J+kk	LIST(4*I+3)
k*J—kk	LIST(4*I—3)

It is important to note the restrictions which these rules impose: A(I+1) is acceptable, but A(1+I) is not! Similarly, you may write X(6*L), but to write X(L*6) is inviting trouble. So observe the rules *exactly*. Some Fortran systems will, in fact, allow you to 'bend' the rules and to use more general arithmetic expressions as subscripts—check with your local manual.

Standard Fortran does *not* permit the use of *subscripted subscripts* such as ANT(K(J)).

To sum up, then:

1. Variables may be subscripted when it is required to manipulate arrays of numbers.
2. Up to three subscripts may be used, but individual computer systems may impose a limit.
3. The subscripted variable takes the general form (in the two-dimensional case):

   variable name (row number, column number)

4. The subscripts must be integer variables, constants or arithmetic expressions. If the latter, they must be constructed in strict accordance with the rules for forming such expressions.
5. The value of the subscript must never be less than one.
6. Subscripted subscripts are not permitted.

Matrices and vectors

The terms *matrix* and *vector* are specialist terms used by mathematicians, scientists and others, and may usually be taken to be synonymous with two-dimensional and one-dimensional arrays respectively.

The DIMENSION statement

When a Fortran program makes use of subscripted variables, it is necessary that the correct amount of memory space is reserved for the elements of the array which are to be manipulated. The purpose of the DIMENSION statement is to ensure that this is done. Let us reconsider the man sorting letters whom we met in Chapter 2.

Before he is able to sort the letters, he must have somewhere to put them—a set of pigeonholes. Further, the holes must be labelled so that it is known exactly which letters are where.

In the same way, before it is able to process data the computer must have somewhere to put it—we call this the machine's memory, or store. The store is divided up into 'pigeonholes' known as *memory cells*, or *store locations*, and each of these is usually able to contain one number or instruction. In order that the individual memory cells can be identified, each one has associated with it an *address*, like the labels on the man's pigeonholes. One of the jobs of the compiler is to ensure that for each variable name used by the programmer a memory cell, or a set of memory cells (for an array), is set aside, and that it is possible at any time during compilation of the program to associate the correct cell or cells with each variable name.

With unsubscripted variables there is no problem—a memory cell is reserved for each variable as its name is encountered during the compilation process. In the case of subscripted variables, however, a little more care is needed. Suppose we have a variable called ALPHA which is subscripted. How will the compiler know the number of memory cells which should be reserved to contain the elements of the array ALPHA? ALPHA might have two elements or it might have 2000. Here is where the DIMENSION statement comes into the picture: its purpose is to ensure that the compiler knows just how many memory cells to put aside for the use of each array used by the program. Suppose that the array ALPHA is single-dimensioned and has thirty elements. This information is given to the compiler by one DIMENSION statement, which will look like this:

```
DIMENSION ALPHA(30)
```

and which must appear in the program *before any other reference to the variable ALPHA*.

The word DIMENSION must be spelt out in full, exactly as shown above. Any number of arrays may be *declared* in a single DIMENSION statement. As an example, suppose that our program has three arrays to deal with, and that their names are VOLTS, AMPS and NODES. Suppose also that they are all two-dimensional, VOLTS having two rows and thirty columns (often expressed as 'VOLTS is a 2 × 30 array'), AMPS is similar in size to VOLTS—2 × 30—and NODES is a 7 × 30 array. The appropriate DIMENSION statement, which would appear at the head of the program, before any other reference to the three arrays, would be:

```
DIMENSION VOLTS(2,30), AMPS(2,30), NODES(7,30)
```

Notice the commas which separate the individual *array declarations*. The order in which the arrays are declared is unimportant.

This statement, then, informs the compiler that it should reserve a sufficient number of memory cells to contain all the elements of the arrays named in it. In this case, 2*30 = 6 elements for VOLTS, and a similar number for AMPS, and 7*30 = 210 elements for NODES. The total requirement is thus 330 memory cells, and all the information needed for this calculation is given in the DIMENSION statement. The subscripts given in the DIMENSION statement must be the maxima which are likely to be used during the execution of the program: it would be no good to declare DIMENSION A(6) and then, later in the program, attempt to work with A(9)!

In the next chapter we shall consider the ways in which arithmetic can be specified in Fortran. First, however, try these exercises to consolidate what you have learned about constants and variables.

Exercises

1. Express the following Fortran real numbers in exponential form:

(*a*) −107.9
(*b*) +0.00397
(*c*) 2522000000.0
(*d*) −0.196
(*e*) +3.973
(*f*) −2920.0

2. The following numbers are expressed in exponential form. Rewrite them in their more familiar form. For example, −.29E−1 would need to be rewritten as −0.029.

(*a*) +.219E−3
(*b*) −.8169E−6
(*c*) 0.3222E+5
(*d*) +.0213E0

3. The following were intended as real variable names, but a few mistakes have been made. Find those which are *incorrect*, and say why they are wrong.

(*a*) POINT
(*b*) LABEL
(*c*) 3NTK
(*d*) A3967
(*e*) REGISTER
(*f*) K1
(*g*) FAR23
(*h*) TA+32

4. Some of the following integer subscripted variables are formed incorrectly, whereas others are correct. Find those which are *wrong*, and give reasons.

(*a*) K2(94)
(*b*) J(2,2,2,2)
(*c*) AT(1)
(*d*) KK(65.2)
(*e*) J(4−I)
(*f*) NODE(4,3)
(*g*) M6(5)
(*h*) LOAD(A)
(*i*) LOAD(J(K))
(*j*) INDIVIDUAL(4,4)
(*k*) M4(6,2,2
(*l*) NAME(6,5)

5. Refer to Fig. 3.4 and write down the subscripts of the following elements of the array:

   (*a*) Buffer stock of item 5
   (*b*) Weekly demand of item 1
   (*c*) Price of item 2

   Identify the following elements of the same array:

   (*d*) TABLE(3,1)
   (*e*) TABLE(4,5)
   (*f*) TABLE(3,3)

6. A is a 6 × 17 array, GAIN is a 3 × 4 array, D and DATE are arrays of dimensions 3 and 6 × 2 × 2 respectively. If all four arrays are to be used in a single program, write the appropriate DIMENSION statement.

7. What are the errors in the following two DIMENSION statements?

   (*a*) DIMENSION A(2,2) BETA(7) N(16)
   (*b*) DIMENSON C(30)

4 Communication and arithmetic

Up until now we have considered some of the basic principles of programming, the drawing of flowcharts, and the forms taken by constants and variables in the Fortran language. We have said little about the way in which arithmetic is performed, or about the way in which the program is made intelligible to the computer. In this chapter, we shall first discuss the main physical medium which enables us to communicate with the computer—the punched card—and then go on to consider the methods of specifying what arithmetic operations are to be performed.

At the moment, and for the foreseeable future—although a great deal of thought is being given to the matter—no equipment is generally available which is able to read handwritten material directly into the memory of a computer. Nor, except in the most primitive manner, is the direct input of human speech possible. Consequently, when we wish to present information to the computer, it is necessary to encode it in such a way that it can be interpreted by electromechanical devices. The commonest of these is the punched card reader, whose medium is the eighty-column punched card. Each alphanumeric character is allocated a unique pattern of holes in a column, and these patterns are punched automatically when the text is typed on a machine called a *keypunch*, which has a more or less standard typewriter keyboard. Punched paper tape is also a popular medium for the input of programs and data, and the direct encoding of information on to magnetic tape and disks is one of the latest developments in the data processing field. Fortran, however, has evolved around the punched card and owes several of its eccentricities to the medium, so we shall consider other forms of input only fleetingly. We shall also assume that output is to a high-speed printer, producing a line at a time, or is punched into cards. A special case is magnetic tape, used as backing storage, and we shall have more to say about this when input and output are dealt with formally in a later chapter.

What, then, is a punched card, and how is it used? Physically, it is a sheet of thin card, normally $7\frac{3}{8} \times 3\frac{1}{4}$ inches, having one corner cut off to facilitate the stacking of a *deck* (or *pack*) of cards such that they are all the same way up. The cards are read by a *card reader*, which passes on to the computer a series of electronic signals derived from the patterns of holes in each column which represent alphanumeric and special characters. The cards will be read one at a time from the top of the deck downwards—that is, the order in which you would read them. The cards will be stacked in the deck, ready for input, face upwards, with the printed side exposed (many keypunches print a readable copy of their contents along the top edge to help the programmer interpret the information).

Fig. 4.1 is a picture of a typical punched card. You will see that it is divided along its longer side into eighty columns. We shall designate the left-most column as column 1, and the right-most column will be known as column 80. Cards may, depending on the use to which they are to be put, bear special printing or coloured marks. These are to help distinguish them for the human user—the computer is only interested in the patterns of holes which they contain. Only in special circumstances can a computer input device recognise marks similar to normal print—magnetic ink is used on cheques, for instance, and the banks' data processing equipment is capable of reading the markings; other installations have optical character readers, but the print has to be specially formed and is not particularly easy for the human eye to interpret without some practice. We shall confine our considerations to information transfer by means of holes in cards—probably the commonest means of input to computers.

In addition to the eighty columns, it should be noted that each column contains twelve rows, ten of which are numbered from 0 to 9. There are two rows above these, known by many different names. The top row is called the 12, + or R row, depending on which manufacturer's equipment you are using, and the second row is known as the 11, – or X row respectively. There are other names less commonly used—a ridiculous state of affairs, but one which does not seem to cause too much confusion. In this text, the top two rows will be referred to as the 12 and 11 rows respectively.

Each column will contain a hole pattern representing a single character. Numeric characters are represented by a single hole punched in the column. For instance, to punch the character '7' in colum 29, we should punch a single hole at the point of intersection of column 29 and row 7. For alphabetic information it is necessary to punch more than one hole in a column: the letter 'A' is produced by punching a hole in the 12 row and, *in the same column*, another hole in the 1 row. For special characters it may be necessary to punch up to three holes in a column, but more than this number are rarely used. The hole patterns of the Fortran character set are shown in Fig. 4.1.

Once the program has been written, the actual punching of the cards is a straightforward clerical operation which can be performed by keypunch operators—usually girls—who know little or nothing about programming. It is very important, therefore, that all work to be keypunched should be very clearly written so that transcription errors are not made at this stage. The finished cards should also be checked by eye after punching to ensure that there are no errors which will be passed to the computer. Such checks, though rather tedious, can save a lot of expensive computer time. To aid this process, even if the keypunch used does not print the characters along the top of the card, there are other

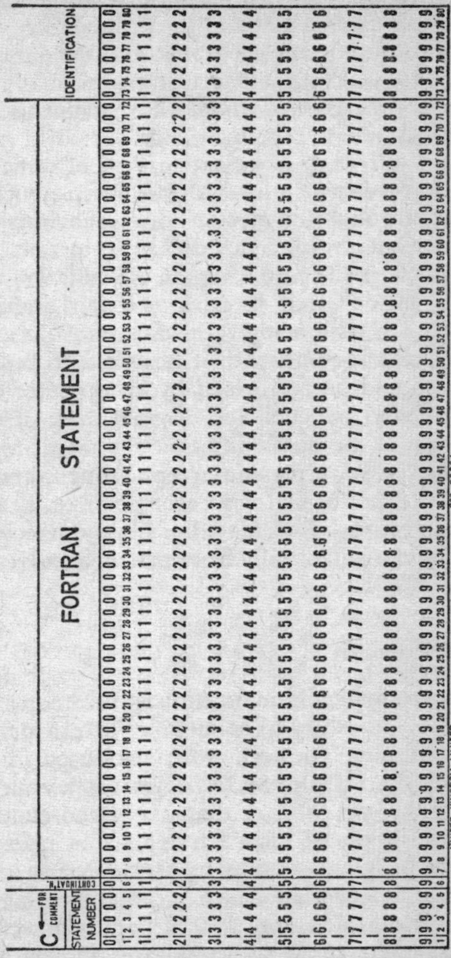
C ← FOR COMMENT
STATEMENT NUMBER
CONTINUAT'N
FORTRAN STATEMENT
IDENTIFICATION
IBM UNITED KINGDOM LIMITED

Fig. 4.1

machines called *interpreters* which will read the cards after they have been punched and add the printed interpretation.

The cards for important programs, and the data for programs which are working satisfactorily, are usually checked by a process known as *verification*. The machine used, called a *verifier*, looks like a keypunch and is used in much the same way. In this case, however, instead of punching the cards, it takes cards which have already been punched. The operator goes through the motions of re-punching the card deck, and if what she punches differs from that which is already punched on the card, then the machine will warn her that an error has occurred, by flashing a light and jamming the keyboard. The card being verified can now be examined more closely, and re-punched if it turns out to be in error. Verification should be performed by an operator different from the one who punched the original deck of cards, if possible, to avoid the possibility that she might repeat her own errors. Even so, errors do creep through, and an eye check should be performed whenever possible. If a card is found to be in error, it is usually difficult and uneconomical to correct it, and it will usually be re-punched *and re-verified.*

The Fortran statement

Before the problem of communication is studied in any more detail, it will be necessary to define the Fortran *statement* a little more carefully. The term was introduced in the last chapter, when the DIMENSION statement was described. In general terms, we can say that a Fortran statement is usually a description of the next step to be taken in the execution of a program—it may be considered as a form of instruction but is generally much more embracing than a machine-language instruction. In terms of the flowchart, the effect of a single box, or even several boxes, may be achieved with one Fortran statement. For example, one might have a box which contains the order: 'Set N equal to zero'. As a Fortran statement, this would probably be written:

N = 0

This is an example of an *arithmetic* statement—one which specifies an arithmetic operation to be performed. The DIMENSION statement is a member of a whole family of *specification* statements, which give instructions to the compiler about such matters as the organisation of memory which will be necessary when the program is executed. The latter are known as *non-executable* statements, for their prime function is organisation, whereas those which perform the actual calculations and other manipulations of data are known as *executable* statements.

It is quite important to distinguish between the two. There are rules for the formation of all these statement types, and these will be given in due course. The statements may be considered to be the sentences of the Fortran language. Let us now have a look at the way in which they are made available to the computer for processing.

Fig. 4.2 shows the general layout of a card used in the preparation of Fortran programs. Often, a computer installation will supply specially printed cards for Fortran programs, and these may have the words 'FORTRAN STATEMENT' printed across the top. But it does not matter if none of these cards is available, since it is the holes in the cards which count, not the information printed on them. The positioning of the Fortran statement on the card is very important and must be carefully noted. If statements are not positioned exactly, even though they may be syntactically correct, the compiler will usually report that the statement is in error. This is because certain constituents of the statement are expected to be in specific places on the card, and most compilers are not sufficiently flexible in their analysis to be able to allow for slight divergences from this

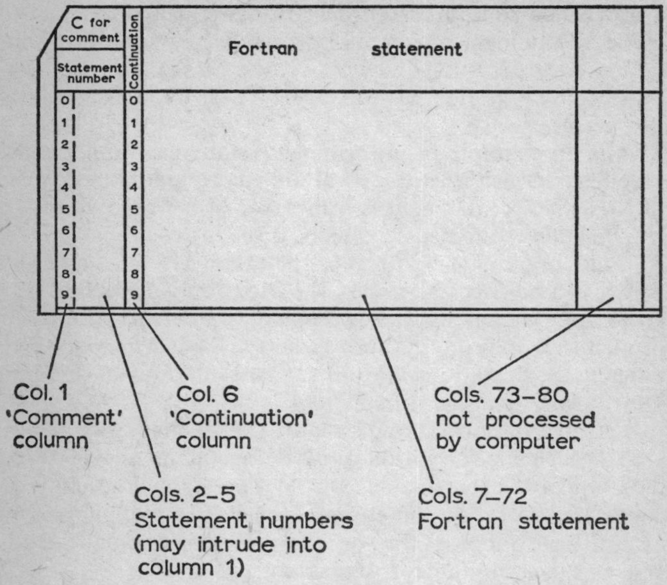

Fig. 4.2

expectation. In this way, we get fast and efficient compilers. More flexibility would result in slower working.

The most important rule is that *there may not be more than one Fortran statement on a card.* This applies even if a statement occupies only a very small portion of the card—such as the statement:

N = 0

which was considered earlier. This could take up as few as three columns of an eighty-column card if blanks were omitted—as they may be. Nevertheless, the remaining columns must be left blank, at least as far as column 72. In all cases, columns 73 to 80 may contain any information at all. This part of the card is ignored by the compiler. Many people like to give each card a *sequence number* so that the cards may be reordered correctly if the deck is accidentally jumbled. Such numbers may safely be punched in these last eight columns on the card.

Let us now consider the layout of the card in detail, with reference to Fig. 4.2 as required.

Column 1

This is the so-called *comment* column. It will normally be blank, but it may contain the letter 'C'. If it does contain a 'C', this is an indication from the programmer to the compiler that the contents of this card constitute a comment—descriptive information about the program and its organisation, designed to help users of the program better understand its construction. Such information will be printed when the program is compiled, but will be completely ignored by the compiler. This is an extremely valuable feature.

Columns 2 to 5 inclusive

This set of columns, usually termed the *statement number field*, will generally be blank, but it may contain a number.

When a program contains decision points, it will often happen that a set of Fortran statements has to be executed in an order other than that in which they appear in the card deck. Or it may be required that a group of statements be repeated many times in a loop. In such cases it will be necessary to branch from one statement to another which does not follow it in the normal sequence. This implies that statements can be identified by some means, so that the statement which initiates a branch can specify exactly the whereabouts of the next statement to be executed. In Fortran, this is achieved by allocating a *statement number* to any statement which is branched to. Thus one might write GO TO 29 in the program, which would cause a branch to the statement numbered 29.

It is not necessary to number all statements, nor is it desirable. Statements are numbered to clarify the flow of a program. If they all bear numbers, this aim is not going to be achieved. Only those statements which are referenced by other statements need be numbered.

Statement numbers need not be sequential, but they must all be different in any program. The first statement in a program, for example, could be numbered 2034, while the second is labelled 27. It would, however, be quite wrong, and unacceptable to the compiler, to have two or more statements numbered 2034 in any one program.

The range of acceptable statement numbers is determined by the compiler being used. In theory, numbers in the range 1 to 99999 may be used, extending back into column 1 if necessary. Statement numbers less than 1 are not permitted. This is another case where the manual should be consulted to establish what is the local practice. Note also that statement numbers are always whole numbers, without a decimal point.

Column 6—the continuation feature

Earlier, the possibility of a statement's being too long to be held on a single card was mentioned. Column 6 provides the answer to this problem. When we write a letter which needs more than one sheet of paper, we usually would continue on another sheet. At the top of the continuation sheet, it is usual practice to write a number, so that the reader will know which is the first sheet and the order in which the sheets are to be read. Much the same is true in writing long Fortran statements: if a statement is too long to fit onto a single punched card, it may be continued on another. The first card of such a statement is distinguished by having column 6 contain either a blank character *or* the digit 0. Subsequent *continuation cards* must have in column 6 a character *other than* a blank or a zero. The presence of this continuation marker in column 6 indicates to the compiler that this card is a continuation of the statement from the preceding card. The characters which are used for continuation may be any in the Fortran character set. Commonly the letter 'C' is used, or the asterisk, '*', but the most logical system would seem to be that of placing a '0' in the continuation column of the first card of the statement and the digits '1' to '9' in column 6 of successive continuation cards. If there are more than nine continuation cards, the alphabetic characters may be brought into use. The number of continuation cards allowed depends on the compiler being used, though the ANSI standard specifies nineteen.

The statement body

The main body of the statement will be contained between columns 7 to 72 of as many cards as are required to hold it. Most statements will fit comfortably onto one card, but the continuation feature may have to be used occasionally. Very rarely, if ever, will the maximum permitted number of continuation cards need to be exceeded, but if this situation does arise it is probably due to poor statement design on the part of the programmer. A little thought will usually show how the original statement can be rewritten as two or more which will fit the formation rules.

You will recall that it has been previously stated that spaces may be freely used to improve the readability of the program. It should be emphasised that this is true only of the *program* statements, and that the form of the *data* expected by the program is much more rigidly defined.

When punching a Fortran statement, not more than one character can be punched in a column. The term 'character' includes the digits 0 to 9, the capital alphabetic letters A to Z and the special characters, such as +, *, etc., shown in Fig. 4.1. The decimal point is a character in its own right, and so a real number such as 29.0 will occupy *four* columns, *not three*. How many columns would be needed if the value were of integer type?

The characters '(' and ')' are, strictly, known as *parentheses* but are quite often referred to as 'brackets'. We shall use the more correct term. Parentheses occupy one column each, just like any other character. What is the minimum amount of space needed to contain the subscripted variable DATA(KA)? The answer is eight columns, of course. Note, however, that it might have been written in many other ways, introducing spaces at any point: DATA (KA), DATA (KA), D A T A (KA) are all equally acceptable, and would need more space on the card.

Let us briefly summarise what has been said about punching Fortran statements onto punched cards.

1. Column 1 is used to identify comments, and may also be used to hold the first digit of a statement number.
2. Columns 2 to 5 will normally contain the statement number, if any. Only those statements which are referred to by others need to be numbered. The statement number may appear anywhere within the statement number field —there is no need to make sure that all statement numbers are aligned on the right or left of the field, though the appearance and readability of the program are improved if this is done.
3. Column 6 is the continuation column. If a card is used for continuing the statement from the preceding card, it should contain a non-zero, non-blank character in column 6.
4. Columns 73 to 80 are not used by the Fortran compiler, and may be used by the programmer for any purpose. It is usual to punch sequence numbers in this field.

Before we go any further, try the following short test. All the answers will be found in the previous section.

1. How many columns are there on the standard punched card?
2. How many of these are used by the Fortran compiler?
3. How many statements can be placed on a single card?
4. How many characters may be punched in a single column?
5. If a statement were too long to fit onto one card, could it be continued on another card? If so, how would you set about it?
6. Some of the following statements are true, others are false. Determine those which are true and those which are false. When a statement is false, give your reason for believing this to be the case. The answers are given after the last question.

(*a*) A Fortran statement starts in column 1.
(*b*) Column 1 is used to contain the first digit of a statement number or a comment indicator.
(*c*) All statements must be numbered.
(*d*) The Fortran statement extends from column 7 to column 80.
(*e*) Column 6 is the continuation column.
(*f*) Spaces may not be left between Fortran characters.
(*g*) Each character must have a column to itself.
(*h*) A Fortran statement must always start in column 7.
(*i*) Small (lower case) letters may be used in Fortran.
(*j*) The identification field (columns 73 to 80) may not be left blank.

Answers to question 6

(*a*) False. A statement may start anywhere on the card other than column 6 or beyond column 72. If it is numbered, the statement number must appear between columns 1 and 5 inclusive. If it is not, the first character must appear between columns 7 and 72 inclusive.

(*b*) False. A statement intended as a comment will certainly have a 'C' in column 1, but the first digit of a statement number need not, necessarily, appear in that position on the card. If the statement number has five digits, the first digit *must* appear in column 1.

(*c*) False. Only those which are referred to elsewhere.

(*d*) False. It must not extend beyond column 72, and the statement number may start as early as column 1.

(*e*) True. This is where the contination marker is placed.

(*f*) False. Spaces may be freely used to improve readability.

(*g*) True. Try it and see!

(*h*) False. See comments on 6(*a*) and 6(*d*).

(*i*) False. Capitals only are allowed.

(*j*) False. Columns 73 to 80 may contain anything. It makes sense to use them for sequence numbers, especially in large program decks.

Finally, a few comments on the handling of punched cards will not be out of place here. When carrying and manipulating cards, always be careful not to damage the edges of the cards. Storage of cards should be in a dry and dust-free place. When the cards are read by machine, two readings of each card are usually performed, and the card will be rejected if the result of the second reading operation differs from that of the first. A typical reason for such rejection is that the keypunch has produced holes which are slightly out of alignment, in which case the machine will need attention.

Comments and continuation

We are very often likely to need to make comments in our programs, if only to be able to identify them and decide what should be happening at some later date. We might, for example, wish to start off a program with the remark: 'This program computes the values of the first 100 terms of a Fibonacci series'—you will remember that we developed an algorithm for this in Chapter 2. Such a comment would be valuable in identifying the program, and we should probably want to make comments at other points in the program—to indicate what each section of each routine is intended to do, for example.

So we have the comment feature in Fortran. Basically, all that has to be done is to place the letter 'C' in column 1 of the comment card: the comment itself will then appear anywhere on the rest of the card. It will not matter if it overlaps into columns 73 to 80, unless these columns are in use for sequence numbers. The presence of a 'C' in column 1 informs the compiler that the remainder of the information on the card is not really required by the program but is only present as an aid to the user. The continuation facility does not apply when we are dealing with a number of consecutive comment cards, though such an arrangement is quite common. In such a case, each card must be marked as a comment with a 'C' in column 1.

Cards which contain comments have no effect at all on the execution of the program. The comment will be printed out at compile time, and so will appear on the program *listing*—the copy of the program which is printed whenever the program is compiled. Many systems, to save time and paper, allow the output of a listing to be suppressed by the user, a feature of particular value when a program is tested and in regular use.

Here is how the Fibonacci comment, mentioned above, might appear:

```
C *** THIS PROGRAM COMPUTES THE VALUES ***
C *** OF THE FIRST 100 TERMS OF A       ***
C *** FIBONACCI SERIES                  ***
```

Asterisks have been used deliberately to make the comment stand out from the rest of the program, but this is not at all necessary.

Here is another example of the start of a program:

```
C DIGITAL COORDINATED TRANSIENT
C EVALUATION SYSTEM  –  ATLAS ONLY
C MAXIMUM NUMBER OF NODES 950
C MAXIMUM NUMBER OF ARRESTER
C CHARACTERISTICS               10
C MAXIMUM NUMBER OF ENTRIES IN
C NCAA                         100
        DIMENSION V(2,950), C(2,950), D(35),
        1              NCAA(7,100), NCA(7,975)
        . . . etc.
```

The comments are being used to indicate what the program's limitations are. The program proper, as far as the compiler is concerned, starts with the DIMENSION statement. The program would function just as well without the comments —their value is to the user. Note the use of the continuation facility in the DIMENSION statement, though it was not strictly needed. Many programmers prefer the following construction:

```
DIMENSION V(2,950), C(2,950), D(35), NCAA(7,100)
DIMENSION NCA(7,975)
```

Multiple DIMENSION statements are quite permissible, and many programmers feel that it is poor style to split a statement of this type by using the continuation feature. It's a matter of personal preference, and both methods are correct Fortran.

Arithmetic

Computers are calculating machines of a sophisticated nature and so any instructions which we give them will involve arithmetic processes: addition, subtraction, multiplication, division, comparison of values. In Fortran, we indicate to the computer exactly what process we want performed by expressing it as a formula rather like an algebraic equation. In addition to the pure arithmetic, we also need to have the facility for making decisions as to which instruction to obey next, and it is here that the digital computer differs from the conventional desk calculator. In this section, we will examine some of the ways in which the arithmetic process to be performed is specified in Fortran.

The basic arithmetic operations are indicated in, more or less, the conventional manner: '+' is used to indicate addition, '—' for subtraction; we have been introduced already to '*', which is used to specify multiplication, and division is indicated by a slash, '/'. Thus, if we wished to divide the variable D by 4.379, this would be written in Fortran as:

D/4.379

(By the way, what is the type of D: real or integer?)

The assignment statement

At first glance, this looks like an equation:

N = N+1

At second glance, it looks like rubbish, for by following elementary rules of algebra it simplifies to:

N−N = 1
i.e. 0 = 1

Well, the first glance must have misled us—maybe it was not an equation after all. And, of course, it wasn't. It was a Fortran *arithmetic statement*, specifying an operation to be performed. The character '=' is *not* an equals sign, and the expression is *not* to be read as 'N is equal to the sum of N and 1'. In fact, '=' is known in Fortran as the *assignment operator*, and the correct interpretation would be the instruction 'Assign to N the sum of the values of N and 1'. In other words, if the initial value of N were 3, the resulting value of N would be 4; if N started out as 77, its value after the assignment would be 78, and so on. Strictly, this was an arithmetic assignment *statement*, probably the commonest type of Fortran statement.

Another way of thinking about it is to say 'is replaced by' when we see the '=' character, thus: 'N is replaced by N + 1'.

Of course, it is not necessary that the same variable should appear on both sides of the assignment operator. Here are some more examples of simple arithmetic assignments:

```
M = 3
L = 14
K = L+M
```

A precise statement of the meaning of the last example is: 'Replace the value currently held in the variable K by the sum of the values held in the variables L and M'. The previous two statements have set the values in M and L to 3 and 14 respectively, so that the final value allocated to K will be 14+3, i.e. 17.

Now you try. The following are two sequential assignment statements from a program:

```
M = 3
M = 2*M + 14
```

What is the value which has been assigned to the variable M after these two statements have been executed?

The answer is 20.

First, the value in M, whatever it was, is replaced by 3. You may like to think of the value '+3' being placed into the box in memory labelled 'M'. Then a copy of this value is taken, multiplied by 2, and 14 is added to the result. The final value resulting from this calculation is then copied back into M, replacing the value which was already there. In this case, the new value is 20.

Notice that there is only one variable name to the left of the '='. This is a very important point; after all, we can only do one thing at a time.

The left-hand side (the part on the left of the assignment operator, '=') of a Fortran assignment statement must be a single variable. It may not be an expression.

The variable may be subscripted, if desired.

It follows that a statement such as A = B + C is quite valid, but one such as B + C = A is not acceptable. Note this carefully—it is a common source of errors for newcomers to high-level languages.

The Fortran arithmetic statement is usually very similar in form to the algebraic formula from which it is derived, but there are a few important differences caused primarily by the fact that all the information must be contained *on* the line, and excursions above and below the line are not possible. Here is an example: to convert the old British currency, pounds, shillings and pence, into pounds the appropriate formula was

$$\text{POUNDS} = \text{P} + \frac{\text{S}}{20.0} + \frac{\text{D}}{240.0}$$

where P is the number of pounds, S is the number of shillings and D is the number of pence, all in the amount to be converted to give a final result, POUNDS.

When this is rewritten as a Fortran assignment, it looks like this:

```
POUNDS = P + S/20.0 + D/240.0
```

Notice a very important basic difference between this statement and that considered earlier:

```
M = 2*M + 14
```

Look carefully at the right-hand side of each statement. Do you see that, where we are dealing with real quantities, *all* the quantities are of real type, and where we are dealing with integer quantities, *all* the quantities are of integer type? Thus, M is found in conjunction with 2 and 14, an *integer* variable with two *integer* constants; in the other expression, we find P, S and D in conjunction with 20.0 and 240.0, three *real* variables used with two *real* constants.

In general, all the terms of the expression on the right-hand side of a Fortran arithmetic assignment should be of the same type (or mode). That is, they should be either all real or all integer.

There are three exceptions to this rule, one of which you have already met. Can you think what it might be? Mixed modes are permitted for subscripted variables, though not within the subscript expression itself. So we may have a real variable with a subscript, and the subscript must be of integer type. A(I) would be an example of this. But A(I+2.0) would not be permissible, because it has a mixed-mode subscript.

Similarly,

X = D(45)/E(N)

would be quite valid, whereas

X = D(45)/M(N)

would not. It is the name of the subscripted variable which determines its type. In this case, D is real and M is integer. We have a mixed-mode condition.

Just as a variable or a constant has a type, or mode, so does the expression which contains that quantity. An expression built from real quantities is said to be of real mode, one built from integer quantities is of integer mode. Although mixed-mode expressions are not permitted, it is allowed that the mode of the right-hand side of an arithmetic statement may differ from that of the variable on the left-hand side. The result of doing this is interesting, and can occasionally be useful.

If the modes of the two sides differ, all calculations will be performed using the mode of the right-hand side, but the final result will have the mode of the *left-hand side*. Let us look at an example to make the process a little clearer.

A = 5.6
A = 3.0*A + 9.3

The value of A after these calculations have been performed will be 26.1—you will find it useful to check the calculation. Now suppose that we had the following two statements instead:

A = 5.6
K = 3.0*A + 9.3

What will be the final value of K? It cannot be 26.1 again, for integer variables can take only whole-number values. So what shall it be—26 or 27? In fact, the value obtained is 26, the nearest integer *below* the computed result, and this is the general rule. There is no question of rounding to the nearest whole number, as often happens in everyday arithmetic. Even if the result were 26.99, its assignment to an integer variable would still give 26 as the final value.

This process can work in the opposite direction. The right-hand expression may be of integer type and the left-hand side a real variable. The effect is to *float* (i.e. convert to floating-point form—the form in which real numbers are held) the result of evaluating the right-hand side. To give an example:

F = 3*K + 4

when K has the value 3 will give for the value of the expression the result 13. Since F is a real variable, the value assigned to it will be 13.0, which is 13 'floated'.

We now have the ability to *fix* (make integer) a real number and float an integer number.

Incidentally, you should take careful note of the use of the multiplication operator, '*'. This may *never* be omitted, even though it is common algebraic practice to do so. The following examples of algebraic expressions and their equivalent Fortran should help to clarify the construction.

Conventional expression	Fortran expression
$ax + b$	A * X + B
$\frac{a + b}{c}$	(A + B)/C
$\frac{a}{b} + \frac{c}{d}$	A/B + C/D
$\frac{(a + b)}{(c - d)}$	(A + B)/(C – D)

Notice the use of parentheses to clarify the meaning of the expressions.

Exponentiation

This is the process whereby a number is raised to a power. When we square a number, we say we have raised it to the power 2: a becomes a^2. When we cube a number, we say we have raised it to the power 3: b becomes b^3. We understand, of course, that a^2 is an abbreviation for $a * a$, and b^3 is an abbreviation for $b * b * b$. In general, x^n is said to be the nth power of x, and represents the number $x * x * x * \ldots$ in which the number of times x appears is n. The figure which is written above the line, and which specifies the power to which the number has been raised, is called the *exponent*. It is also possible to have fractional exponents: $p^{5/2}$ is an alternative way of writing the square root of p^5. We could equally well have written it as $p^{2.5}$. So much for the mathematics—what about the Fortran?

For a start, we cannot write using superscripts. And we cannot put the exponent into parentheses, because we already use them to contain subscripts. So we introduce a new operator—the exponentiation operator '**'—a double asterisk. Thus where, in normal algebraic notation, we would write 5^2, in a Fortran arithmetic expression this would be written as either 5 ** 2 or 5.0 ** 2, depending on whether our 'five' was fixed or floating-point (i.e. integer or real). In fact, the exponent could have been written as a real number, but for integer powers this has a tendency to introduce inaccuracy and also to take longer to execute, so expressions like 5.0 ** 2.0 are best avoided. In any case, it is much better to do the arithmetic yourself, before submitting the program to the computer, when there are simple numerical expressions to be included. In this case, it would be more efficient to use either 25 or 25.0, rather than have the machine work it out. The more usual application of exponentiation is that in which one or more variables are involved:

```
V(17) = S(4) ** 4
Q = P ** 2.5
Z = Y ** X
```

and so on.

Note, however, a couple of important rules about exponentiation:

1. Only a *real* variable may be raised to a real power.

   ```
   Y ** 0.3 is permitted
   K ** 0.3 is not.
   ```

2. A negative number, *whether it is real or not*, may not be raised to a real power. This saves our getting into the messy region of complex numbers and having to take the logarithms of negative numbers. How would *you*, as a Fortran compiler, deal with something like (−1.0) ** 0.5? Faced with an exponentiation involving a real power,

most Fortran systems attack it this way: Let the expression be X ** Y. We can evaluate this by using logarithms. In everyday work, we should probably use logarithms to the base 10 (ordinary log tables), but it is more usual for a computer to work with logarithms to the base *e* (2.7182818 . . .). But the principle is the same. We calculate antilog$_e$(Y * log$_e$X). An alternative way of writing this is $e^{Y * \ln X}$, since ln (or even just plain log) is understood to mean 'log$_e$'. Unfortunately, there are serious mathematical problems if X turns out to be negative. If this does happen during the execution of a program, the most likely result is that the machine will print a message to the effect that an error has occurred, it cannot do anything further with your program, and it is going to drop it and go on to the next program. So beware of this condition, and others like it, and ensure that it cannot happen in your programs!

Before continuing, let us consider an example of an arithmetic assignment statement which involves most of what has been covered so far.

DATA is a real array having two dimensions, and it is required that the element in the *n*th column of the ninth row shall be raised to the third power; the variable E is to be divided by 5.97 and then added to the cubed array element. The whole is then to be multiplied by another variable, B, and the result assigned to the third element of the one-dimensional array VAR. Before you look at the solution given below, try and write a suitable statement.

How does it compare with this?

```
VAR(3) = B * (DATA(9,N) ** 3 + E/5.97)
```

Note the use of parentheses. These can usually be used freely to avoid any possibility of ambiguity in arithmetic expressions, and should always be used when in doubt. A knowledge of the order in which arithmetic expressions are evaluated is useful, and is generally on the following lines:

1. All subexpressions involving exponentiation (or unary plus, or unary minus: −X + Y has a unary minus sign in front of X) are dealt with first, in the order in which they appear from left to right.
2. Next, all multiplications and divisions are dealt with, in the same way.
3. Additions and subtractions are performed, again in order from left to right.
4. *But:* all parenthesised expressions are fully dealt with first, and where such expressions are nested the innermost ones are evaluated first of all.

Nested parentheses are sets of parentheses one within the other, like these: ((( )))

The order of evaluation of our assignment statement will thus be:

1. Raise DATA(9,N) to the power 3
2. Divide E by 5.97
3. Add the result of step 1 to that of step 2
4. Multiply B by the result of step 3
5. Assign the result of step 4 to VAR(3), replacing whatever value might be there already.

A useful check on the syntactic correctness of an arithmetic expression containing parentheses, whether as algebraic brackets or as subscript delimiters, is to count the numbers of left-hand and right-hand parentheses. They should be equal, or *balanced*, and the compiler will very quickly object if it discovers one of your statements has 'unbalanced parentheses'.

There is no limit, within the physical limitations of the punched card and the computer system you are using, to the complexity of the arithmetic expressions you are allowed to build in Fortran. That is not to say that you should try to make your statements as complicated as possible! The simpler the better, in general, for the program becomes much easier to understand if it progresses in straightforward steps rather than in great leaps and bounds, and this will be found a great help when you come to find the errors in a program which is producing unexpected results. Later, of course, when some experience has been gained, the rules may be bent a little, but it is best to hasten slowly in this frustratingly fascinating subject.

One last word, and then you can try the exercises. There will usually be more than one way of writing a Fortran arithmetic statement. Here are some examples of different ways of writing the same basic formula:

```
PRICE = A + B/20.0 + C/240.0
PRICE = A + C/240.0 + B/20.0
PRICE = A + 0.05*(B + C/12.0)
PRICE = A + (B + C/12.0)/20.0
```

All are equally valid.

Exercises

1. True or false?

(*a*) Fortran cards must have the characters both punched and printed on them.
(*b*) The maximum number of continuation cards which may be used is four.
(*c*) The last column in which Fortran information can be punched is column 72.
(*d*) A statement may be numbered zero.
(*e*) In some cases, two characters can be punched in one column.
(*f*) There should not be more than one Fortran statement to a card.

2. What would be the numerical result of executing the following sequences of statements?

   (*a*) A = 3.0
   F(9) = A**2 + 3.46
   What is the value of F(9)?
   (*b*) W = 1.25
   P = 5.0 * (W/5.0 + 1.0)
   What is the value of P?
   (*c*) NUMBER(K) = 5
   ALPHA = (NUMBER(K)**3
   What is the value of ALPHA?

3. It is required to write an assignment statement for the following calculation:

   Subtract 3.9 from the variable A, and raise the difference to the power 3. Multiply the result by another variable, B, and divide by 5.6. The final answer is to be assigned to a variable BETA. Determine which of the following statements are *wrong*, and give reasons for your decisions.

   (*a*) BETA = (A – 3.9)**3 * B/5.6
   (*b*) BETA = (3.9 – A)**3 * B/5.6
   (*c*) BETA = (A – 3.9) * B**3/5.6
   (*d*) BETA = B * (A – 3.9)**3/5.6
   (*e*) (A – 3.9)**3 * B/5.6 = BETA
   (*f*) BETA = B/5.6 * (A – 3.9)**3
   (*g*) BETA = A – 3.9**3 * B/5.6

4. Write a Fortran statement equivalent to the following algebraic formula:

$$E = \frac{3.479dp^2}{5.67 + Q}$$

5. Write a Fortran statement for the following formula:

$$Y = 8X^3 + 7X + 4.3X^2$$

6. Can you see a way of rearranging the formula of question 5 so as to give a quite different Fortran statement?

7. Use the values given to evaluate the following Fortran arithmetic expressions:

   (*a*) J * (K – 2 * L)/6 + J**2
   where J = 2, K = 10, L = 2
   (*b*) 4.0 * (B/(2.5 * C))**2 + 3.0
   where B = 10.0, C = 2.0
   (*c*) (F * (F – G))/(V – 3.5)
   where F = –5.0, G = –3.0, V = 5.5
   (*d*) A * B/C**D
   where A = 1.0, B = 4.0, C = 4.0, D = 2.0

8. What will be the final value of K in the statement sequence below?

```
ALPHA = 5.5
K = 2.3 + 2.0 * ALPHA
```

9. The following statements have syntactic errors which render them invalid. What are the errors?

   (*a*) K = A**2 + M(4)
   (*b*) CARD = (ALPHA * 7.93 + V/(5.8 * DATA(9,8))/8
   (*c*) N + 14 = B(9,9,3)
   (*d*) CALCULATION(4) = H * 5.679
   (*e*) B = C + * TH(7,9)

10. Rewrite the given Fortran statement as its equivalent everyday algebraic form.

```
KK(3) = 2 * (MN(5)**2 – N(4))/N(4)
```

5 Control statements

When, in Chapter 2, flowcharts were discussed, you will recall that there were, basically, two types of box joined together by flowlines. The boxes were called event boxes (rectangular in shape) and decision boxes (diamond shaped). Event boxes generally correspond to assignment statements, or sequences of assignments, but the decision boxes are those which will concern us here. These decisions determine the logic flow of the program. They have a controlling function, and the Fortran statements which implement them are known as *control statements*. With their aid we shall be able to introduce branching and loops into our programs.

There are several control statements, and each has its own set of rules governing its use. It will often happen that the functions of two or more of these statements will overlap—it is usually possible to perform decision-making operations in a number of different, though equally valid, ways, depending on the preference of the individual programmer. There is style in programming as in all creative pursuits. It follows that there will rarely be one correct way of programming the solution to a specific problem.

Before getting down to the detailed description of the control statements, and the ways in which they are used, it should be emphasised that, *in the absence of instructions to the contrary*, the executable statements of a Fortran program are executed sequentially—that is, in the order in which they were originally written down. The word 'executable' is used deliberately, for some statement types do not fall into this category. All assignments and the control statements are of the executable type.

The GO TO statement

This is the first and the most straightforward of the control statements which we shall consider. It has the general form:

GO TO *xxx*

where *xxx* represents any statement number.

It works in the following way: the Fortran program is executed, statement by statement, until the GO TO statement is reached; the next instruction executed will be that whose statement number appears in the GO TO statement. The section of program given below should help you understand the action more clearly.

```
      KAFD = 5.097 * DELTA(N)
      GO TO 15
   14 KAFD = KAFD + 1
   15 XD(KAFD) = 1.0
```

The value 5.097 * DELTA(N) is first computed (as a real value) and is fixed by being assigned to the integer variable KAFD. The statement GO TO 15 is then encountered and specifies that the next statement to be executed will be that numbered 15, *not* that numbered 14 even though it is the next in the program sequence. Statement number 15 might have occurred almost anywhere in the program, either before or after the GO TO statement, since there are no restrictions as to the number of statements which may be jumped over. It is important to ensure that the statement number which appears in a GO TO statement is that of a statement elsewhere in the program, and an executable statement at that! The compiler will soon tell you if it is not, but this is time-consuming and poor programming practice. Do your own checking.

Another point worth noting is that the statement immediately following a GO TO statement should have a statement number. A little thought will reveal the reason for this:

imagine what would happen if the statement following the GO TO in our example did not have the label 14. Statements would be executed sequentially until the GO TO was encountered, and control would then be transferred to that labelled 15. Consequently, the statement immediately following a GO TO can never be reached unless it bears a statement number. In the example, it is labelled 14, and we assume that somewhere else in the program there will be a GO TO 14 statement. As you may have noticed, without confusion I hope, the terms 'statement number' and 'label' are often used synonymously.

This statement type is usually referred to as an *unconditional branch*, since the transfer of control must be made unconditionally. There are *conditional branch* facilities also, which will be dealt with later, which help in the construction of program loops. But before going on to that topic, there is another form of the GO TO statement worth considering.

The 'computed' GO TO statement

The occasion often arises that there is a choice of statements to be executed next in a program, the particular one taken depending on some previous calculation. For instance, a program may be divided into three sections dealing, possibly, with women in the categories 'married', 'single' and 'divorced', and the choice of which section should be executed is determined by a code number held in a variable —let's call it INDIC. Thus, if the value in INDIC were 1, we might select the section of the program dealing with married women. Suppose the first statement of this section is labelled 10. If INDIC has the value 2, we might select the section of program concerned with single women, and the first statement of this *routine* could well be labelled 20. Finally, the third section, dealing with divorced women, might be labelled 30 and selected by a value of 3 in INDIC. But how is the selection to be made? The computed GO

TO statement gives us all the facilities we need and, for this example, would look like this:

```
GO TO (10, 20, 30), INDIC
```

Expressed in words, this statement means: 'If INDIC has the value 1, go to the statement labelled 10. If INDIC has the value 2, go to the statement labelled 20. If the value of INDIC is 3, go to the statement labelled 30.'

In general, the instruction allows control to be passed to one of a number of statements, depending on the value of a *control variable*, here called INDIC.

The general form of the computed GO TO statement is thus:

GO TO (*list of statement numbers*), *control variable*

Statement numbers must be contained within the parentheses, and separated by commas. There must be a comma after the closing parenthesis, and the control variable may be any non-subscripted integer variable—it may not be a constant. The next statement executed is determined by the value of the control variable, *which may not be less than 1.*

If the control variable has the value 1, the branch is to the statement bearing the first label of the list. A value of 5 for the control variable means that the branch is to the statement bearing the fifth label of the list, and so on. The number of statements in the list will be the same as the largest value which the control variable can assume. If a value larger than this turns up, or a zero or negative value, an error condition is assumed to exist, and appropriate action will be taken by the computer system.

The following will give some idea of what a computed GO TO statement should *not* look like. The reasons for their being in error are given beside each.

GO TO 23,24, IB	No parentheses around the list of labels.

GO TO (23,24), K(NC)	The control variable must be a *non-subscripted* integer variable.
GO TO (23,24) J	No comma after the right parenthesis.
GO TO (23,24), RESULT	The control variable must be of type *integer*.
GO TO (23,24.0), K	Statement numbers are always *integers*.

Now try this one: a subscripted integer variable, KATE, can take values of 34, 35 or 36 at one point in a program. If the *n*th element of KATE has the value 34, it is required to transfer to the statement numbered 235; if it has the value 35, we must branch to statement number 574; if the value is 36, a jump to statement number 99 is needed. Write a suitable sequence of Fortran statements to fulfil the requirements, and explain in words what happens during the execution of your sequence. A possible answer is given below.

```
J = KATE(N) - 33
GO TO (235, 574, 99), J
```

J is always equal to the current value of KATE(N), less 33. Hence when KATE(N) has the values 34, 35 and 36, J will have the values 1, 2 and 3 respectively. J may thus be used as the control variable of a computed GO TO statement.

The arithmetic IF statement

This is a true decision-making statement, a conditional branch. Its name gives a clue to the way in which it is used: IF some particular arithmetic condition exists, then perform one operation; IF it doesn't, then perform another operation, and so on.

More precisely, this particular statement allows us to

transfer control to any one of three statements. The one which is selected depends on the value of an arithmetic expression. Consider the following example:

```
IF (Q) 3, 4, 5
```

Here, Q represents the arithmetic expression whose value will determine the next statement to be executed (variables and constants are the simplest examples of such expressions). The expression is contained within parentheses. Following it are three statement numbers, separated by commas. These identify the possible statements for execution.

Any arithmetic expression will have a value, which may be less than zero, equal to zero or greater than zero. The statement whose number appears first will be executed if the value of the parenthesised expression is negative; that whose number appears in the second position will be executed if the expression has a value of zero; the statement identified by the last number is executed if the expression has a value greater than zero.

So the statement may be interpreted in the following way:

IF the value of the variable Q is
negative: GO TO 3
zero: GO TO 4
positive: GO TO 5

But remember that the parentheses (which are essential) may contain *any arithmetic expression.* Here is another example:

```
IF (A – 3.4) 10, 11, 12
```

If (A – 3.4) is negative—in other words, if the value of A is less than 3.4—a branch will be made to the statement labelled 10. If the value of A is equal to 3.4, and thus (A – 3.4) is equal to zero, the branch will be to the statement labelled 11. If A is greater than 3.4, a branch to statement number 12 will be executed.

So the general form of the arithmetic IF statement is:

IF (*any arithmetic expression*) s_1, s_2, s_3

where s_1, s_2 and s_3 are statement numbers. Note that *three* statement numbers are required, but they need not all be different. The positions of the parentheses and the commas are invariable.

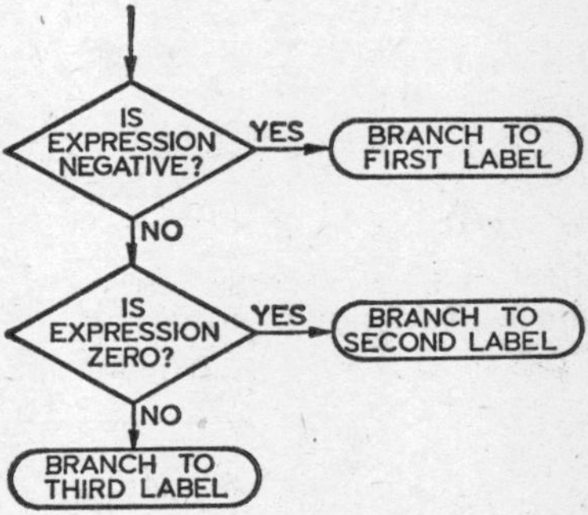

Fig. 5.1

Fig. 5.1 is a flowchart to illustrate the arithmetic IF statement, and you will see that the three-way nature of the branch is clearly demonstrated here. However, it can be used as a two-way branch by having two of the statement numbers in the statement the same.

As an example of this application of the arithmetic IF, suppose that there exists a variable, VAR(7). If VAR(7) has a value less than or equal to 15, it is required to branch to the statement labelled 71. If, however, VAR(7) has a value exceeding 15, the branch is to be to label 4. Write an appropriate arithmetic IF statement, and then compare it with that given below.

IF (VAR(7) – 15.0) 71, 71, 4

The logical IF statement

The arithmetic IF statement gives us a three-way branch determined by the evaluation of an arithmetic expression. There is another type of IF statement—the logical IF—which provides a two-way branch facility determined by the evaluation of a *logical* expression, and it often turns out that this is an easier statement to use. It is certainly more economical of labels. Here is an example to give a general idea of the appearance of the statement:

```
IF (A .EQ. B) GO TO 56
```

Notice the appearance of a new operator—.EQ.—in this statement. This is a *relational* operator—one which serves to establish a relationship between two Fortran quantities. Here, the relationship is one of equality, and the expression in parentheses should be read as: 'A is equal to B.' The whole statement thus becomes: 'If A is equal to B, go to label 56.' The expression 'A .EQ. B' is called a logical expression. It is an expression which can have only one of two possible values. These are not numerical values but *logical values*, *true* and *false*. If A is, in fact, equal in value to B, the expression 'A .EQ. B' is true; if the values of the variables differ, the expression is false. There are only two possibilities.

If the logical expression in parentheses is true, the statement which follows immediately after the right parenthesis (in this example, GO TO 56) will be executed. Often it will be a GO TO statement, but it is not necessary that it should be. The only important type of statement that it may *not* be is another logical IF statement.

If the logical expression turns out to be false, the statement after the parentheses is *ignored completely* and the computer goes on to the next statement in the normal sequence as if nothing had happened. The values of the variables which appear in the logical expression are unchanged, whether the result of its evaluation is true or false.

There are six relational operators altogether, and a list of them follows:

.LT.	is less than
.LE.	is less than or equal to
.NE.	is not equal to
.EQ.	is equal to
.GE.	is greater than or equal to
.GT.	is greater than

The dots before and after the letters serve to distinguish them from ordinary variable names, and *must not be omitted.*

In addition to the relational operators, which enable some very effective and elegant conditional statements to be composed, there are three *logical operators*, used to combine simple relations together into more complicated logical expressions. These are best illustrated by example, so consider the following.

If the value of X is less than or equal to that of another variable, Y, and at the same time is greater than that of a third variable, Z, the value 1.0 is to be assigned to the fourth variable, ABLE. Otherwise, if the conditions cannot be fulfilled, the value of ABLE is to be left unchanged.

This could certainly be done using an arithmetic IF, but several statements would be needed. One approach might be this:

```
  IF (X – Y) 1, 1, 2
1 IF (Z – X) 3, 2, 2
3 ABLE = 1.0
2 next statement
```

But using the logical features of Fortran we can get by with a single statement:

```
IF (X .LE. Y .AND. X .GT. Z) ABLE = 1.0
```

Besides the saving in the number of statements to be written, such a logical IF statement is easier to understand at first glance. The above example might be interpreted as: '*If* X is less than or equal to Y *and* X is greater than Z, *then* set ABLE equal to 1.0.' The symbol '.AND.' as used here is a logical operator, used to join two relational expressions—a very common occurrence. The whole logical expression will have the value *true* only if *both* the expressions joined by .AND. are true.

Another logical operator is the symbol '.OR.', which is used in much the same way, except that an expression involving it will be true if *either* of the expressions it joins is true. Our example can be changed slightly to illustrate the use of .OR.

If the value of X is less than or equal to that of Y, or if it is greater than that of Z, assign the value 1.0 to the variable ABLE. Otherwise, assign the value 2.0 to ABLE.

Try this one yourself, and then look at the solution below. To help a little, here is the equivalent expressed using the arithmetic IF statement:

```
   IF (X – Y) 20, 20, 10
10 IF (X – Z) 30, 30, 20
20 ABLE = 1.0
   GO TO 40
30 ABLE = 2.0
40 next statement
```

Both these solutions are worth detailed examination:

(*a*)
```
   IF (X .LE. Y .OR. X .GT. Z) GO TO 10
   ABLE = 2.0
   GO TO 20
10 ABLE = 1.0
20 next statement
```

(*b*)

```
ABLE = 2.0
IF (X .LE. Y .OR. X .GT. Z) ABLE = 1.0
next statement
```

Solution (*b*) is perhaps the more elegant, though it involves the cancelling of an assignment if the required conditions are fulfilled. You may have written something like this:

```
IF (X .LE. Y .OR. X .GT. Z) ABLE = 1.0
ABLE = 2.0
next statement
```

and be wondering where you went wrong. After all, you made the test and gave both alternative courses of action in the right places—or did you? In fact, the final result of this sequence will *always* be to assign the value 2.0 to ABLE. Remember how the logical IF works: when the logical expression is true, the statement immediately to its right is executed, and when that has been done, the normal sequence continues. So, unless the right-hand statement is a GO TO, the next one executed after a successful IF statement will be the one on the line below. Often, of course, it *will* be a GO TO statement, and a branch will be made to another part of the program. Fig. 5.2(*b*) is a flowchart of this (wrong) solution which should make the reason for its being in error obvious. The other diagram (Fig. 5.2(*a*)) is a general picture of the working of the logical IF statement.

A further point about the logical IF: mixed-mode relational expressions are not permitted any more than mixed-mode arithmetic expressions. So if you write something like IF (A .LE. K) . . ., for instance, you may confidently expect the compiler to give you an error indication.

Finally, one last logical operator. The symbol '.NOT.' has the effect of negating the result of evaluating a logical expression—if the result would have been *true*, a value of *false* is produced, and vice-versa. Thus .NOT. (A .EQ. B) is equivalent to (A .NE. B), and may occasionally be useful

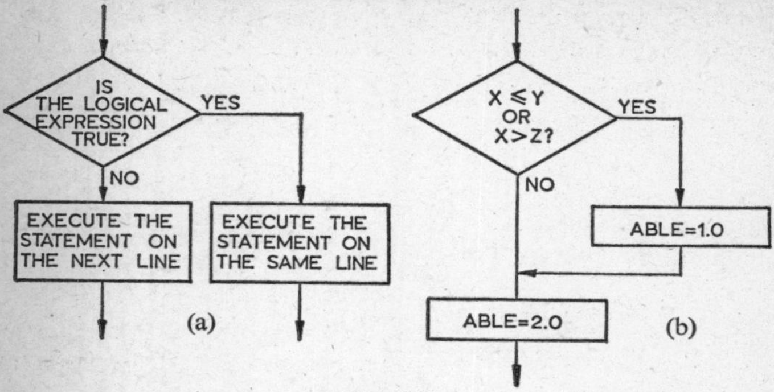

Fig. 5.2

to make a program less involved than would otherwise be the case. Note that logical expressions may contain parentheses to prevent ambiguity, and the order of application of operators is:

1. .NOT.
2. .AND.
3. .OR.

It follows that the expression:

A .EQ. B .OR. C .NE. D .AND. E .GT. F

will be taken to mean

A .EQ. B .OR. (C .NE. D .AND. E .GT. F)

Program loops

There are now enough Fortran features available to enable fairly realistic program segments to be written, and any real application of a computer is likely to contain loops.

Suppose it is wished to form the sum of the first fifty natural numbers, that is: $1 + 2 + 3 + \ldots + 49 + 50$.

You may remember that you drew a flowchart for this process as an exercise at the end of Chapter 2. A flowchart for the main part of the program is given in Fig. 5.3, and the

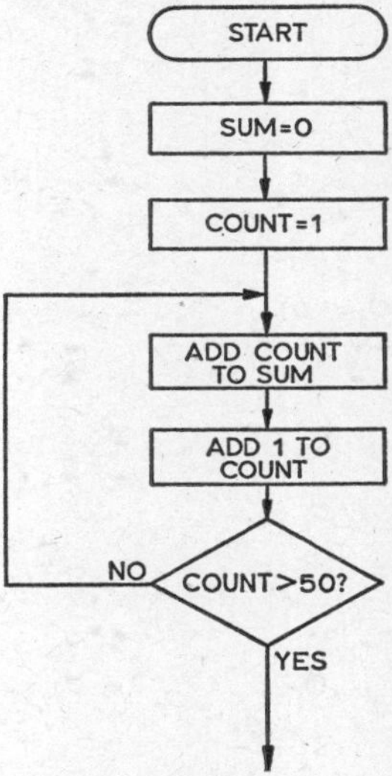

Fig. 5.3

equivalent Fortran statements are given below. There are three versions of this routine, using different features of the Fortran language.

(*a*) Using the arithmetic IF

```
      ISUM = 0
      KOUNT = 1
   10 ISUM = ISUM + KOUNT
      KOUNT = KOUNT + 1
      IF (KOUNT - 50) 10, 10, 20
   20 next statement
```

The first point to notice here is that the names of the variables have been adapted to suit the initial letter requirements of the Fortran language. Thus, the total being accumulated will be held in the variable ISUM, not SUM which would be the name of a real variable. Since all the values to be dealt with are integers, it is better to hold them in integer variables. Similarly, the other variable is not COUNT but KOUNT, K having been chosen as the initial letter to ensure that the convention is not broken. Note how the loop is established by attaching a label (10) to the statement which is the first of the group to be repeated.

(*b*) Using the logical IF

```
   ISUM = 0
   KOUNT = 1
10 ISUM = ISUM + KOUNT
   KOUNT = KOUNT + 1
   IF (KOUNT .LE. 50) GO TO 10
   next statement
```

In this example, only one label is necessary. The same naming conventions are used as in (*a*) above.

(*c*) Using a DO loop

```
   ISUM = 0
   DO 30 KOUNT = 1, 50, 1
30 ISUM = ISUM + KOUNT
   next statement
```

You will have noticed that this routine is constructed in an entirely new manner. But it achieves exactly the same result as the others.

Let us examine this new facility in detail.

The DO loop

This is one of the most used features of the Fortran language since it considerably simplifies the setting up of program loops. The major problems facing the programmer organising a loop are 'housekeeping chores'—jobs not directly concerned with the problem to be solved but which are necessary to ensure that the calculation proceeds smoothly. The initialisation of the counter (KOUNT, in our example), the changing of its value by regular amounts each time round the loop and the testing which is needed to discover the point at which to leave the loop—all these are housekeeping chores. The purpose of the DO loop construction is to minimise the amount of housekeeping which the programmer has to concern himself with.

Let us look back to example (*c*) above and analyse it to demonstrate the working of a DO loop.

The first statement has the effect of clearing the variable ISUM ready to receive the additions which will finally accumulate to the required sum.

At each stage of the calculation, there is only one central process to be considered: the incrementing of ISUM by the next integer in the series. The statement labelled 30 represents this central process in general terms, KOUNT being the current value of the next integer to be added in. This statement needs to be repeated fifty times, with the value of KOUNT varying in steps of 1, from 1 to 50, before the final exit from the loop is made.

Now look at the second statement of the routine:

```
DO 30 KOUNT = 1, 50, 1
```

Put into words, this is equivalent to saying: 'Execute all the statements which follow this line up to and including that labelled 30, making sure that KOUNT has the value 1 to start with. Then increase the value of KOUNT by 1 and, so long as the new value does not exceed 50, repeat the sequence starting with the statement immediately following the DO statement. Continue to do this until the value of KOUNT exceeds 50, at which point go to the next executable statement *after* that labelled 30.'

There are four numbers in the DO statement: the first is always a statement number, and identifies the last statement in the *range* of the DO—that is, the last statement of the group to be repeated; the numbers after the '=' sign represent, respectively, the initial, final and increment values for the control variable—KOUNT, in this case. The control variable is that whose name appears before the '=' sign. The commas must appear exactly where they are shown, except when the amount by which the control variable is to change is 1, when the last ' , 1 ' may be omitted. This is a time-saving feature, since the commonest increment is, in practice, 1. So our example may be rewritten thus:

```
DO 30 KOUNT = 1, 50
```

and will have exactly the same effect.

The general form of the DO statement is:

DO *xxx i* = *initial value*, *final value*, *increment*

xxx represents a statement number. It is the number of the last statement of the group to be repeated—the last in the range of the DO. It may never be a variable.

i is the control variable. It must be of integer type, and must not be subscripted.

initial value is the value assigned to the control variable at the beginning of the loop. It appears in the statement as a non-subscripted integer variable or constant.

final value is the value the control variable will assume in the last execution of the loop. Again, it appears as a non-subscripted integer variable or constant. When this final value is exceeded, the looping process will cease, and control will be passed to the statement immediately following the last of the loop.

increment is the amount by which the value of the control variable is increased each time round the loop. When this has the value 1, it may be omitted.

It is important to note that the initial value, final value and increment must always be positive integer values—they may never assume the value of zero or become negative. As with all the other Fortran statements we have dealt with, any number of spaces may be left between the various elements of the DO statement.

Here are a few examples of correct and incorrect DO statements. Study them carefully.

Correct:

```
DO 307 JA = 2, 60, 2
DO 2 M = 1, J, 5
DO 64 K = 1, N
DO 19 KATE = 2, 72, LB
```

Incorrect:

DO 294 J = 2 150 N	No commas between the DO parameters (the constants and variables to the right of the '=' sign).
DO NAN J = 1, K	The statement number may not be a variable.
DO 469 A = 1, MA, 7	The control variable must be integer type.
DO 64 KKT = 34, 6, –2	None of the DO parameters may be negative, including the increment.
DO 79, JA = 1,8	No comma should be given after the statement number.

The range of a DO statement—that is, the group of statements which comes between the DO statement itself and the final statement which is identified by the statement number in the DO statement—may be as large as you like. Any of the normal Fortran operations can be performed inside a DO loop, including, as we shall see, other DO loops.

Let us consider another example of the use of a DO loop. We shall write a program for the conversion problem which was discussed in Chapter 2. The flowchart is given in Fig. 2.6. At the moment we are not able to instruct the computer to read in data and print out results—this will have to wait until the next chapter. We can, however, write the Fortran statements which will perform the arithmetic and set up the loop structure. Perhaps you would like to try this before looking at the suggested solution given below?

```
      DO 23 N = 1, 2000
   23 HEIGHT = 0.0254 * (XI + 12.0 * F + 36.0 * Y)
      next statement
```

As soon as N exceeds 2000, the iterative (repetitive) process will be terminated, and control will pass to the statement following that labelled 23.

Ending a DO loop

The way in which a DO loop is ended is very important. The golden rule is never to terminate a loop with a branch statement, conditional or otherwise. It would be incorrect, for instance, to write something like this:

```
    5 DO 24 KK = 1,29
      B(KK) = E * D(7)
   24 GO TO 17
```

The computer will set KK equal to 1, work out a value for B(1) and then pass to statement number 24. What can it do now? Statement 24 specifically orders a branch to statement number 17, somewhere else in the program. On the other hand, KK should be incremented (by how much?) and the loop repeated. An error will be indicated, either by the compiler or at the time of execution. In either case, the required results will not be obtained.

The CONTINUE statement

Sometimes it is necessary to put some form of decision-making statement at the end of a DO loop. We might, for example, want to put a computed GO TO at the end of a loop so that we could branch out prematurely if certain conditions were fulfilled. Logically, the computed GO TO statement ought to be the last statement in the loop, but if it is written in that position the resulting program will be invalid. What can be done? The answer lies in a very useful feature of the Fortran language—the CONTINUE statement.

This is a rather odd statement when first encountered, since its execution accomplishes absolutely nothing. It has the effect of transferring control to the next statement in the normal sequence. If it occurs as the last statement of a DO loop, the next statement in the normal sequence is either the first statement in the range of the DO or the one immediately following the CONTINUE statement, depending on the value of the control variable. The CONTINUE statement constitutes a *dummy* event, which can be used anywhere a labelled executable statement may appear in a program. Since it is not, strictly, a branch, it may legitimately appear as the last statement in the range of a DO loop.

Its general form is:

xxx CONTINUE

where *xxx* is a statement number. Some programmers always terminate their DO loops with a CONTINUE statement—it saves their having to remember what types of statement they may *not* use in that position. Yet others attach all their labels to CONTINUE statements, claiming that it makes for easy alterations to the program when needed. Again, it's a matter of style. There are certainly some computer systems that produce more efficient code from Fortran DO loops which terminate on a CONTINUE statement.

We could rewrite the DO loop we used originally as an example of the use of the CONTINUE statement:

```
      ISUM = 0
      DO 30 KOUNT = 1, 50
      ISUM = ISUM + KOUNT
   30 CONTINUE
      next statement
```

This will have precisely the same effect as the original statements. There is no real need to use the CONTINUE statement here, but look at the routine which follows:

```
      DO 9 K = 3, NB, 3
      ARR = B(17)**4 + D(K)
      IARR = ARR + 1.0
      GO TO (9, 10), IARR
    9 CONTINUE
   10 next statement
```

In this example, it is assumed that the value of IARR will normally be 1, in which case the looping operation will proceed in the usual way. If, however, IARR ever attains the value 2, an exit from the loop will be made—a perfectly permissible action—to statement number 10.

The CONTINUE statement is essential in this case since the last statement in the range of the DO must, logically, be a computed GO TO, and this is not allowed.

More rules

Before passing on to the more advanced uses of the DO loop, one or two general rules for the construction of loops should be learned.

1. It is not permitted to branch, from within the range of a DO statement, to the DO statement itself: all internal branches must eventually lead to the terminal statement. This implies that a routine such as that given below would be invalid:

```
43 DO 45 J = 1, 60
   K(J) = MAS/5 - N(J)
   KA = K(J)
   GO TO (44, 43, 45), KA
44 MAS = MAS + 1
45 CONTINUE
```

   This sequence is incorrect because the GO TO statement refers to the label of the DO statement (43). The compiler should indicate an error condition. Each time round the DO loop, we must ensure that the last statement in the range is executed—it may not be by-passed.

2. Entry to a DO loop must always be via the DO statement itself. It is not permitted to transfer control to a statement which is within the range of a DO from a point outside that range. Here is another example to clarify the position:

```
   A = 1.0/A
   GO TO 16
19 DO 17 K = 1,10
16 WA(K) = A/B(K)
   . . .
17 CONTINUE
```

   The DO statement has here been by-passed. This cannot be allowed, because it is this first statement which establishes the initial and final values of the control variable, and also determines the increment.

3. A very important point in Fortran loops is that none of the values of the loop parameters must be altered, once fixed by the DO statement, within the range of the DO.

So you should never write a sequence of statements such as this:

```
DO 19 I = 1, 36
I = 2 * I
N = N + 1
etc.
```

See how the value of the variable I is being changed *inside the loop*. The value of N is changing as well, of course, but this is acceptable. I, however, is the control variable which was set by the DO statement to vary in a regular manner from 1 to 36. Instead, if the statements are executed as written, the control variable will take the values: 1, 3, 7, 15, 31. This is a rule which is very easily broken, especially when dealing with large loops. It has been responsible for many apparently inexplicable sets of wrong results.

Nested DO loops

Earlier, it was stated that DO loops could be placed within other DO loops. The process of so doing is usually called 'nesting' of DO loops, and the result may be known as a *nest of DO loops* or *a set of nested DO loops*.

Let us consider a specific problem to make the idea clearer. Suppose we have a matrix (two-dimensional array) with ten rows and twelve columns. The problem is to *transpose* this matrix—that is, to form a new matrix which has twelve rows and ten columns, the elements in each row of the new matrix being those which were in the corresponding column of the original. Here are an array and its transpose, of smaller dimensions, just for example:

Original	1	2	3	4	Transpose	1	5	9
	5	6	7	8		2	6	10
	9	10	11	12		3	7	11
						4	8	12

A little study will reveal that the subscripts for any element in the transpose are the reverse of those for that element in the original array. For instance, the element '7' is in the (2, 3) position of the original array and the (3, 2) position of the transpose. Similarly, the element '10' is in the (3, 2) position of the original array and the (2, 3) position of the transpose. This applies whatever the size of the array, and if we name the original 10 × 12 array ARR and its transpose BRR we may say that, in general,

$$\mathrm{BRR}_{k,j} = \mathrm{ARR}_{j,k}$$

for values of k from 1 to 12 and values of j from 1 to 10. (You may not agree with these ranges for k and j. If not, think very carefully and ensure that you know which are rows and which columns.)

Now try writing a flowchart for the transposition of ARR into BRR. A suggested solution is given in Fig. 5.4 overleaf. (*Hint:* your chart will contain two loops.)

Well, this probably looks rather complicated. But careful examination will show that it is really quite straightforward. We start by setting J equal to 1 and enter the major, or outer, loop. Here, K is given the value 1 and the minor, or inner, loop is entered. This contains the central process of transposition:

BRR(K,J) = ARR(J,K)

Since K and J are both equal to 1 the first time round, this is the same as saying:

BRR(1,1) = ARR(1,1)

K is now increased by 1 (to give the value 2) and a check is made to see whether it exceeds the maximum allowed value, namely 12. This test fails, and the inner loop is repeated. Since K has changed, the effect is now:

BRR(2,1) = ARR(1,2)

Execution of the inner loop continues, with the value of K increasing by 1 at every stage, until it exceeds 12, when a return is made via the *outer* loop after incrementing J and

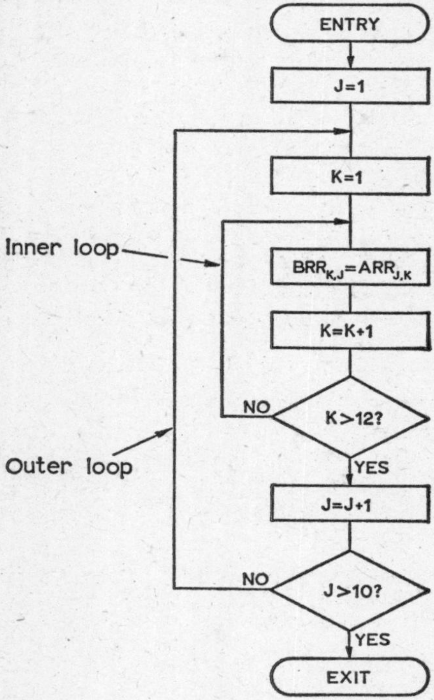

Fig. 5.4

testing for *its* maximum value, 10. J thus becomes 2, the inner loop is re-entered *after resetting K to 1*. So the next assignment will be:

BRR(2,1) = ARR(1,2)

and the process continues as before until K again reaches the value 12. Eventually the point is reached at which K has the value 12 and J has the value 10. Both indices (subscripts) have reached their maxima and the calculation is finished. The central computation will have been performed 120 times (once for each element in the matrix).

A Fortran coding of this flowchart is given below, and illustrates a nested DO loop quite nicely.

```
      DO 10 J = 1,10
      DO 20 K = 1,12
      BRR(K,J) = ARR(J,K)
   20 CONTINUE
   10 CONTINUE
      next statement
```

It is permitted, when a set of nested DO loops terminate at the same point, to make the DO statements refer to the same terminal statement.

The example might thus have been written somewhat more economically (but perhaps less intelligibly) in the following way:

```
      DO 1 J = 1, 10
      DO 1 K = 1, 12
    1 BRR(K,J) = ARR(J,K)
```

Where extreme clarity of program organisation is needed, it is often helpful to indent the range of a DO, except for the DO statement itself and its terminal statement. That might produce the following from our example:

```
      DO 10 J = 1, 10
            DO 20 K = 1, 12
                  BRR(K,J) = ARR(J,K)
   20       CONTINUE
   10 CONTINUE
      next statement
```

If you adopt this method, however, do not indent the statement numbers or there will be trouble!

Remember that the innermost loop will always be entered last and fully executed first. In the above example, the inner loop starts with the statement DO 20 K = 1, 12. This is entered as part of (i.e. after) the outer loop but will be completed first. Usually, the inner loop will be executed completely more times in the course of solving a problem than the outer loop. In the present example, every time that the outer loop's range is executed, the inner loop is completely executed twelve times, with a different value of K each time.

This idea of nesting can be extended so that three, four or more loops can be contained one inside the other. There is no formal limit to the *depth* of nesting which is allowed, but individual computer systems are likely to impose their own. As you might expect, there are some specific nesting rules which must be adhered to if trouble is to be avoided.

Loops which are to be nested must be completely contained within one another and must not be allowed to overlap. This is illustrated in Fig. 5.5, which shows, on the left, an example of a valid DO loop nest.

Each of the lines defines the range of one DO. Notice that the lines do not cross each other as do those of the invalid example which is shown on the right.

An example of a set of invalid Fortran statements which breaks this rule is given below:

```
      DO 29 I = 1, 24
         D(I) = A * R(I, 2)
         DO 30 K = 1,5
   29 A = A + 1.0
   30 C(K) = 0.0
```

Look at this example carefully. You will see that the two DO loops overlap each other. The result is meaningless—try it and see.

Before we leave the DO loop, it should be noted that the value of the control variable ceases to be defined after the loop has reached its natural termination. In other words, you should not rely on the control variable's having any particular value when a loop terminates normally. It may have the value you expect, or one more than you expect, or

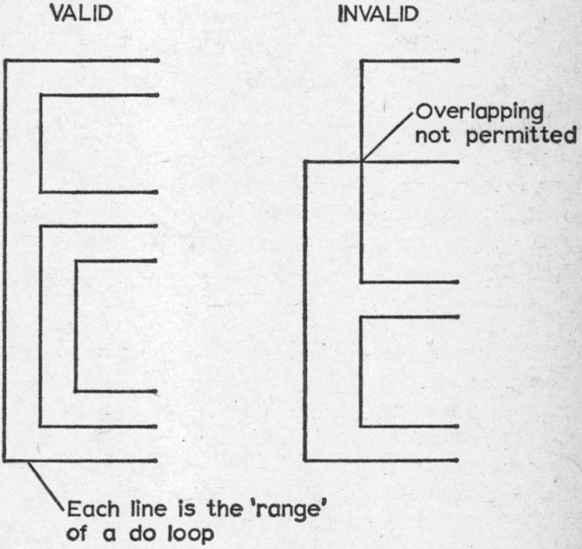

Fig. 5.5

any old value. Don't depend on it. This applies only to a normal exit from a loop which has finished its execution. If a branch is made out of a loop before it has finished, the control variable will have the value to which it was set at the beginning of the last time round before the branch.

Thus, after executing:

```
   DO 10 I = 1,10
      Z(I) = X(I) + Y(I)
10 CONTINUE
   next statement
```

when 'next statement' is executed, the value of I is unknown. But after executing:

```
      DO 10 I = 1, 10
         Z(I) = X(I) + Y(I)
         IF (Z(I)) 10, 20, 10
   10 CONTINUE
      GO TO 30
   20 next statement
```

if, in the third loop, the value of Z(I)—that is, Z(3)—turns out to be 0.0, a branch out of the loop to label 20 will be made and the value of I will remain at 3. Let us now write a program which incorporates some of the features which have been discussed in this chapter.

A simple program

A market research team has interviewed 5000 housewives about their margarine preferences. They have been asked to compare the brand under test with a similar brand in the same price group and state whether they think it is better than, about the same as or inferior to the other brand. Each person interviewed was awarded a score of +1 if she thought that the test brand was worse than the other make, +2 if she considered them both to be about the same and +3 if the test brand was rated better than its competitor.

In order to assess the appeal of their product, the manufacturers of the test margarine wish to know the percentage of women in each group. Our job is to write a program which will analyse the 5000 replies and produce the required percentage figures.

For the time being, we shall ignore the input of data and the output of the final results. These will be the subject of the next chapter. Let us assume that the replies are held in the one-dimensional array DATA, which has 5000 elements.

The value of each element will thus be 1, 2 or 3, depending on the preference of the housewife concerned. We shall also define three variables, BETTER, SAME and WORSE, which will finally contain the required percentage values.

The method used will be to examine each of the entries in DATA in turn and to decide whether the person to whom the entry refers thought that the test margarine was better than, the same as or worse than its rival. Having made this decision, the appropriate variable, BETTER, SAME or WORSE, can be incremented so that, when all 5000 entries in DATA have been examined, these three variables will each contain a count of the replies which correspond with their names: BETTER will contain the count of 'better than' replies, SAME the count of 'same as' replies and WORSE the count of 'worse than' replies. Finally, the three values will be divided by 50 to yield percentages. (For example, if 3000 of the 5000 thought that the product was better, this will represent a percentage of (3000/5000) * 100, which is the same as 3000/50 = 60%.)

Before looking at Fig. 5.6, try to draw a flowchart for the solution to this problem and, using IF and DO statements where appropriate, write a suitable program. A possible program is given below.

```
          DIMENSION DATA(5000)
          BETTER = 0.0
          SAME = 0.0
          WORSE = 0.0
C ***     THE COUNTS ARE NOW INITIALISED
C ***     THE MAIN LOOP STARTS HERE
          DO 40 K = 1, 5000
C ***        DETERMINE VALUE OF NEXT REPLY
             IF (DATA(K) - 2.0) 10, 20, 30
C ***        DATA(K) HAS VALUE 1
   10        WORSE = WORSE + 1.0
             GO TO 40
```

```
C ***      DATA(K) HAS VALUE 2
   20      SAME = SAME + 1.0
           GO TO 40
C ***      DATA(K) HAS VALUE 3
   30      BETTER = BETTER + 1.0
   40 CONTINUE
C *** WE NOW HAVE THE SUMS. NEXT, THE
        PERCENTAGES
C     BETTER = BETTER/50.0
      SAME = SAME/50.0
      WORSE = WORSE/50.0
```

Notice the liberal use of comments. The groups of asterisks (***) are used only for emphasis—they make it easier to identify the comments, but are not necessary. Indentation is also used to improve readability.

How does your version compare? Did you remember the DIMENSION statement? Note carefully the use of GO TO and CONTINUE statements. It has been assumed that the value of an element of data, if it is not exactly 2, must be less than 2 (1) or greater than 2 (3). Many programmers would argue that such assumption involves a risk, in that grossly erroneous data items might not be detected.

The program could be rewritten using only GO TO and IF statements. You might like to try this, discarding the DO loop construction. Here is a possible solution, using a computed GO TO statement, in which the questionnaire responses are held in an *integer* array MARGE.

```
      DIMENSION MARGE(5000)
      BETTER = 0.0
      SAME = 0.0
      WORSE = 0.0
      K = 1
   10 J = MARGE(K)
      GO TO (20, 30, 40), J
```

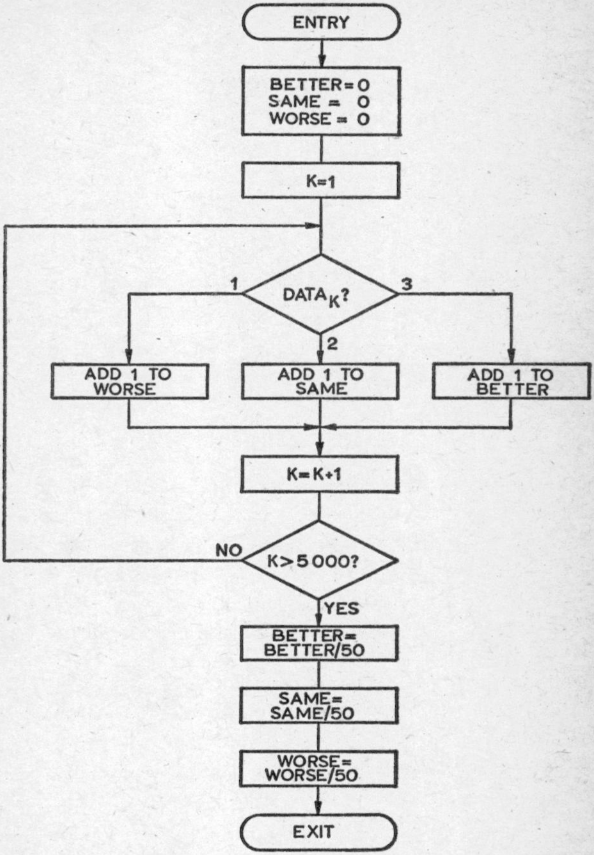
ENTRY
BETTER = 0
SAME = 0
WORSE = 0
K=1
DATA$_K$?
1
2
3
ADD 1 TO WORSE
ADD 1 TO SAME
ADD 1 TO BETTER
K=K+1
K>5 000?
NO
YES
BETTER= BETTER/50
SAME= SAME/50
WORSE= WORSE/50
EXIT

Fig. 5.6

```
20 WORSE = WORSE + 1.0
   GO TO 50
30 SAME = SAME + 1.0
   GO TO 50
40 BETTER = BETTER + 1.0
50 K = K + 1
   IF (K .LE. 5000) GO TO 10
   BETTER = BETTER/50.0
   WORSE = WORSE/50.0
   SAME = SAME/50.0
```

Why did we introduce the variable J? Wouldn't it have been simpler to write GO TO (20, 30, 40), MARGE(K)? If your reply is 'Yes', have another read through the section on the computed GO TO statement!

Now try the following exercises on control statements.

Exercises

1. Say whether the following statements are true or false:

   (*a*) A Fortran program's statements are executed in an order determined by the statement numbers.
   (*b*) The statement which follows a GO TO statement must have a statement number.
   (*c*) Only five statement numbers are allowed in a computed GO TO statement.
   (*d*) The following is a valid Fortran statement:

   ```
   GO TO (45, 97, 998, 56), K34B
   ```

   (*e*) So is the following:

   ```
   GO TO (6, 5, 8, 997, 1), K(13)
   ```

2. A variable is the nineteenth element of the one-dimensional array KA, and can take only values between 454 and 457 inclusive. Branches to statements numbered 12, 13, 14 or 15 are to be made when the value of KA(19) is

454, 455, 456 or 457 respectively. Write sequences of statements to achieve this:

(*a*) using a computed GO TO statement;
(*b*) using arithmetic IF statements;
(*c*) using logical IF statements.

3. Find the errors in the following DO statements:

(*a*) DO 34, I = –4, N, 7
(*b*) DO 67 K = 2, N(4), M(3)
(*c*) DO 56 K = 2.0, 64.0, N
(*d*) DO –23 JK = 1, 78
(*e*) DO 24 A = 1, 19

4. Find the errors in the following IF statements:

```
(a)    IF (A + D**2), 1, 2
(b)    IF (A – 3.9 2, 3, 4
(c)    IF (AR + 34) 6,7,8,9
(d)    IF (A * N(3)) 3, 45, 6
(e) 4  IF (ATH(4) – D(7)**2) 4, 7, 4
```

5. In each of the following examples, write a set of statements which will produce a branch to statement number 1 if the conditions specified are fulfilled, and a branch to statement number 2 if not. For example, if the condition were: A(7) is greater than or equal to 3.97, the statement would be

```
IF (A(7) – 3.97) 2, 1, 1
```

In some cases, more than one statement may be needed. Use any control statements which you think may be suitable.

(*a*) Variable DS(17) is not equal to zero.
(*b*) Variable B(9, 7) is less than or equal to zero at the same time as variable T(9) is equal to zero.

(*c*) K (which may assume any value in the range 1 to 5 inclusive) has a value between 1 and 3 inclusive, and A(4) is less than or equal to zero.
(*d*) T is not equal to S, but the square of T is equal to the cube of V.
(*e*) The value of C differs from those of D, E, F and G.

6. Given a 10 × 10 matrix MAT, write a program to transpose it into the new array MATX, squaring every term of MAT in the process. For example, using smaller arrays,

if MAT = 1 2 3 the result will be MATX = 1 16 49
4 5 6 4 25 64
7 8 9 9 36 81

$$\text{MAT} = \begin{matrix} 1 & 2 & 3 \\ 4 & 5 & 6 \\ 7 & 8 & 9 \end{matrix} \qquad \text{MATX} = \begin{matrix} 1 & 16 & 49 \\ 4 & 25 & 64 \\ 9 & 36 & 81 \end{matrix}$$

7. Given two one-dimensional arrays, A and B, each having thirty elements, write a set of Fortran statements which will form the products of corresponding pairs of elements from the two arrays and add together all the products so produced. Let the result be called SUM. Then we have:

SUM = A(1) * B(1) + A(2) * B(2) + . . .
+ A(30) * B(30)

When SUM has been formed, it is to be tested to see if it is greater than 3050. If it is, generate a branch to statement number 56; if not, then pass control to statement number 45.

6 Input and output

In this chapter we shall consider the methods by which data can be read into the computer's memory under the control of our program, and also the ways in which the results can be caused to be printed after the calculations have been completed.

A complete *job* for the computer will usually consist basically of two parts. The first of these will be a deck of cards containing the Fortran program. The second part is another deck of cards into which has been punched the *data* used by the program to compute its results. Items of data will be read into the computer when the program gives the appropriate instructions. This distinction between program and data is important: the rules for the preparation of Fortran statement cards do *not* apply to data cards. Thus columns 73 to 80 are available for holding items of data, and columns 1 and 6, for instance, have no special meaning.

The results of computer calculation may be presented in many ways and on many media, but the commonest method used by the Fortran programmer is the high-speed line printer. These machines print a complete line of 120 or 132 characters at a time, at speeds of 400 to 1200 lines per minute, typically. An alternative, particularly for the smaller computers, is a device rather like an electric typewriter called a *teletypewriter* ('teletype' for short). Sometimes the Post Office style teleprinter will be found, and electric typewriters proper will be met with on occasion. Answers can also be punched into standard eighty-column cards, or stored on magnetic tapes, disks or drums. They may be punched onto paper tape or even plotted automatically using graph-plotting devices.

Another common output device is the video display unit (VDU), a device similar to your television receiver, on which the results appear written on the screen. This has the advantage of high speed, but there may be problems (of expense, if not technical) in converting the screen image to a *hard copy* on paper.

Our immediate interest is the Fortran statements which will enable us to control the input of data from a card reader, or similar device, and the output of results, in the format which is best suited to our needs, on a line printer or teletype page.

In order to perform an input or output operation, it is necessary to supply the computer with *two* different sets of information. The first specifies the names of the variables involved—those which are to receive the data being read or those which are to have the values they contain transferred to the printed page. The second set of information will define *how* the transfer is to be attacked—where the items of data are on the card or where they will be on the page; whether they are real or integer; how many places of decimals are required for real numbers, and so on.

The READ statement

This is the statement used to read data into the computer's memory. Let us look at an example:

```
READ(2, 12) A, K
```

Every Fortran system will have attached to it a number of different input and output devices, each of which is identified to the program by a code number. In the remainder of this chapter, these devices will be assumed to be a card reader, code number 2, and a line printer, code number 3. The READ statement tells us *what* is being read and *which device* it is being read from, and gives a pointer to an explanation of *how* the information being read is laid out on the card. The interpretation of our example is: 'Read from the card reader two numbers and assign these to the variables A and K, in that order. The way in which the values are laid out on the card is explained in the statement numbered 12.'

Statement 12 will be a non-executable statement called a FORMAT statement. We know its purpose; its structure will be discussed later.

The general form of a READ statement is thus:

READ(*dev*, *xxx*) *list of variable names*

where *dev* is the code number of the device being used for input and *xxx* is the number of a FORMAT statement.

The individual names in the list of variable names are separated by commas. As usual, any number of spaces may be left between the elements of the READ statement.

Remember: the READ statement indicates *what* is to be read, and *where* from; the FORMAT statement associated with it will specify *how*.

Now you try an example. Suppose that there are six variables, U, V, W, X, Y and Z, to which numerical values are to be assigned. These values have all been punched into a card, in the right order. Information as to the exact layout of the card is given in FORMAT statement 34. The card reader is device number 2. Write a suitable READ statement.

(*Note:* Although specific device codes have been quoted in this book, for convenience, the actual codes in use will vary from machine to machine. This is a point which readers with access to a computer should check with their system manuals.)

The answer to the problem is:

READ(2, 34) U, V, W, X, Y, Z

The order in which the variable names appear in the list is very important. This list will be scanned from left to right.

Thus, the first number on the data card (the left-most one) will be assigned to the variable U, V will be assigned the value of the second number on the card, and so on through the list. It follows that if the statement had been:

```
READ(2, 34) V, U, W, X, Y, Z
```

the values of U and V would have been different.

The variable list

The list of variables can be considerably more complicated than we have seen so far. It consists of a number of *list elements*, of which the simple variable we have used so far is the simplest example. Subscripted variables may also be used, and the type may be real or integer. No signs should be attached to variables in the READ list. This does not imply that negative numbers cannot be input: negative signs are quite valid on the data cards being read, but they must not appear in the list of a READ statement. This statement would be invalid:

```
READ(2, 34) +N, -H(9)
```

because of the + and − signs before the variables.

The list should not contain any numerical values—it would scarcely make sense to attempt to assign another numerical value to a constant.

The amount of information which is transferred into memory by a single READ operation is often called a *record.* Every READ operation results in the effective physical movement of at least one card from the input hopper of the card reader to its output hopper, passing through the reader mechanism on the way. The number of cards constituting a record depends on the number of data items to be read and their arrangement on the cards as specified in the FORMAT statement. Very often, however, it will happen that the words 'card' and 'record' will be, in effect, synonymous.

The input of a few simple variables is a fairly straightforward affair, their names simply being listed in the READ statement. Arrays, however, may present a problem. Suppose, for example, that we have to deal with a thirty-element, one-dimensional array called Q. It is required to read values from cards into each of the first fifteen elements of Q. How is this to be achieved?

One possibility would be to write a very long statement:

```
READ(2, 100) Q(1), Q(2), Q(3), Q(4), Q(5), Q(6), . . . Q(15)
```

which would be tedious and poor Fortran style, but it would work.

We might use a DO loop:

```
      DO 10 I = 1, 15
         READ( 2, 100) Q(I)
   10 CONTINUE
```

but, since a record has to consist of at least one card, this would be a little wasteful, since only one number would be read from each card.

If we make the assumption that it is possible to punch five numbers on a card, we might combine the two methods:

```
      DO 10 I = 1, 11, 5
         READ(2, 100) Q(I), Q(I+1), Q(I+2) Q(I+3),
     1      Q(I+4)
   10 CONTINUE
```

which, again, would work but has little to commend it on aesthetic grounds (some people would say this of the Fortran language as a whole!).

In practice, we should probably use the device known as the *implied DO loop*, which sets up a structure very similar to that of the DO loop but using a different mechanism and dispensing with the word 'DO'. This feature is not of general application: it may be used only for input and output lists.

In effect, it is an abbreviated way of writing out the list in full. Here is our example expressed using this construction:

```
READ(2, 100) (Q(I), I = 1, 15)
```

which may be expressed in words as: 'Read, from device number 2 in accordance with the layout given in FORMAT statement 100, values of Q(I) for values of I ranging from 1 to 15, inclusive.'

The effect of this statement is precisely the same as that of the first example. All fifteen elements are read as a single record, since there is only one READ statement to execute. It is possible, as with the standard DO loop, to vary the increment:

```
READ(2, 200) (AD(I), I = 1, M, 2)
```

but, when this is done, it is important to ensure that M has a value before an attempt is made to execute the READ statement.

Implied DO loop list elements may be mixed with ordinary variables in the READ list:

```
READ(2, 101) X, Y, (A(J), J = 1, 20), L, M, N
```

This will have the effect of reading values for X and Y, twenty values for the first twenty elements of the array A, then L, M and N.

Input statements such as the following are quite common:

```
READ(2, 300) N, (X(I), I = 1, N)
```

Here N elements of the array X are given values, N itself being determined by being read from the same record. When this technique is used, it is important that N should be at a point in the list prior to its use as a parameter of the implied DO.

Nested implied DO constructions are quite acceptable:

```
READ(2, 233) ((FLOW(J, K), K = 1, 4), J = 1, 3)
```

This is an order to read values into (FLOW(J, K) for values of K from 1 to 4 inclusive) for values of J from 1 to 3 inclusive. Note carefully the parenthesis structure, which must be observed exactly. Note also that the evaluation is from the inside out: K runs through its set of values before J is incremented, and then the process repeats. The inner loop is in the inner parentheses, and values are assigned in the order: FLOW(1, 1), FLOW(1, 2), FLOW(1, 3), FLOW(1, 4), FLOW(2, 1), FLOW(2, 2), FLOW(2, 3), FLOW(2, 4), FLOW(3, 1), FLOW(3, 2), FLOW(3, 3), FLOW (3, 4). Thus the elements of FLOW have been read in row by row. How would you rewrite the statement to have the elements read in column by column? Don't forget to check that your parentheses balance!

Input of complete arrays

Frequently, it is required to assign values to every element of an array rather than, as in the examples given above, to parts of the array. Given a twenty-element, one-dimensional array, DATA, there are a number of ways in which every element could have a value read into it. One of the simplest would be:

```
READ(2, 111) (DATA(I), I = 1, 20)
```

and this is probably the best approach, since there is no possibility of ambiguity and every element is named in the order in which it will be used.

There is, however, another construction which is often used, and which is almost certain to be encountered in other people's programs. It requires only that the *name* of the array be given in the READ list:

```
READ(2, 111) DATA
```

The compiler is aware, from the previous DIMENSION statement, that DATA is an array, and also that it has twenty elements. It simply generates the appropriate machine instructions to fill all twenty elements with numbers read from cards, in the order DATA(1), DATA(2), . . . DATA(20).

Note that this technique can only be used when the *whole array* is to be processed. If only a part of the array is to be dealt with, then the elements concerned must be named explicitly using one of the methods explained earlier. And, of course, all arrays used *must* be defined in a DIMENSION statement.

One further point is of importance in connection with this shorthand way of reading in an array. The method may be used with two- and multi-dimensioned arrays, but in these cases it is necessary to be familiar with the convention used to determine the order in which the elements are assigned values from the data card. In the case of the two-dimensional array, values are assigned column by column. Thus:

```
READ(2, 444) MAT
```

where MAT is a 3 × 4 array, will assign values in the order:

```
MAT(1, 1), MAT(2, 1), MAT(3, 1),
MAT(1, 2), MAT(2, 2), MAT(3, 2),
MAT(1, 3), MAT(2, 3), MAT(3, 3),
MAT(1, 4), MAT(2, 4), MAT(3, 4).
```

See how the left-most subscript is varying most rapidly. The principle extends to three- and higher-dimensioned arrays: the further to the left in the set of subscripts, the more rapidly the subscript varies. Obviously, this order is very important when data is being prepared for reading by the simplified method, and it must be borne carefully in mind.

The WRITE statement

Just as the READ statement provides for the input of data to the computer, so the WRITE statement allows for the numerical values of programmer-selected variables to be output on a line printer or other *peripheral device*. Much of what has been said about the READ statement applies to the WRITE statement. For instance, it has virtually the same form:

```
WRITE(3, 4) A, B(8), (C(I), I = 1,7)
```

would have the effect of sending the values of A, the eighth element of B and the values of the first seven elements of C to the device whose code is 3—probably the line printer. All this will be in accordance with the FORMAT specified in statement number 4.

Most line printers allow up to 120 characters to be printed in a single line; the larger models can deal with up to 132 characters per line. In practice, when using Fortran, the actual number of characters which can be printed is one less than this—119 or 131—for reasons which will appear later. Printers such as the teletypewriter have about 70 characters to the line. The characters may be any of the Fortran character set, and some systems allow additional special characters to be printed as well.

It is not uncommon to have a WRITE statement with an 'empty list'—that is, with no variables in its list. A statement of this type would look like this:

```
WRITE(3, 6)
```

and would mean that, although it is not required to print the values of any variables, some output is nevertheless needed. We might, for example, want to print out headings, or some other relevant information. The code for the peripheral device, and the reference to a FORMAT statement, will never be omitted.

We may confidently regard the WRITE statement as having exactly the same form, and obeying the same rules, as the READ statement. The ability to output parts (or the whole) of an array using the implied DO loop feature applies equally to the WRITE statement, and complete arrays may be output by supplying the name only. In the latter case, the order in which two-dimensional arrays are output is the same as before—by column—and higher-dimensioned arrays are dealt with in the similar manner described above.

But now we must deal with the FORMAT statement.

The FORMAT statement

This is a non-executable statement whose purpose is to establish the context for the information which is being transferred between memory and an input/output device by a READ or WRITE statement. It may be regarded as setting a background onto which the information will be laid.

In Chapter 3, the representation of numbers was dealt with in some detail, but it will do no harm briefly to review this in view of its relevance at this stage. You will recall that there are basically two types of numeric constant—integer and floating-point, or real, numbers. No decimal point appears in the integer constant, whereas the real constant *must* contain a decimal point somewhere. It was also mentioned that real numbers, although always held internally as floating-point numbers, may be written in either of two ways. These are the normally accepted form, such as 3.456, and the exponential form, of which 0.3456E+1 is an example. These two numbers represent the same value, of course. If you are at all unsure about this, it is suggested that you should turn back to Chapter 2 and refresh your memory.

Basically, the Fortran compiler is a very unsophisticated program, as a rule, and the more help it can be given by the programmer the better. So, on input, we must tell it when to expect integer and when real values. On output the same information is required, together with details of spacing between numbers, number of decimal places, whether the normal or exponential form of numbers is to be used, and many other details. All this information is given in the form of *field specifications* in the FORMAT statement.

The general form of the FORMAT statement is as follows:

xxx FORMAT (*list of field specifications*)

where *xxx* is the statement number which appears in the associated READ or WRITE statement.

There are several different types of field specification, and these will be described in detail in the following sections.

The 'I' field specification

This is used when the information being transferred is of integer type. Let us consider an example of its use which will also illustrate the way in which the FORMAT statement is related to its input or output statement.

Suppose that it is required to read in a value for the integer variable, MA. These statements would do the trick:

```
  READ(2, 1) MA
1 FORMAT (I5)
```

The READ statement should by now be familiar: 'Read a value for MA from the card reader (device number 2) in accordance with FORMAT 1.' Incidentally, it is worth noting that every FORMAT statement must have a statement number, otherwise it cannot be referenced. Here, the reference is to statement number 1, and particularly to the field specification contained within the parentheses:

I5

This tells the Fortran system two things: that the information to be read is of integer type (I), and that it takes up five character positions on the card (5). To be precise, it will occupy the *next* five positions on the card but, since MA is the only item to be read from this card, this implies that the first five columns, 1 to 5, will be used. This number is termed the *field width* of the item being processed, and the actual space taken up by the item is called a *field*. It follows that, as we have specified so exactly where the number will be, we had better make sure that we punch it onto the card in the right place—onto the *data* card, i.e. in the data deck. No data can appear on a FORMAT card. If the number is punched into columns 2 to 6, by accident, instead of columns 1 to 5, a wrong value will be read, for the digit in column 6 will not be 'seen' by the Fortran input routines. Care is the answer, as always: care and checking before execution.

In our example, the field width of five implies that the number will contain five characters. *Not necessarily five digits.* It is *not* required that, if the whole space is not needed, it should be filled up with zeros. Thus, the number 'one' would be punched as:

ƀƀƀƀ1 (ƀ has been used to indicate a 'space' character)

rather than as

00001

though this would be equally acceptable. Blank characters will be interpreted as zeros. So if we were to punch, by mistake,

ƀƀƀ1

a value of 'ten' would be read, using the I5 specification defined above.

An algebraic sign may be included, if desired, but is not needed for positive numbers. So, with a field width of five characters, integer numbers from −9999 to 99999 can be represented. The important thing is that the units digit, or *least significant* digit, should be in the right-most character position in the field. This is known as *right-adjustment*, or *right-justification*, of the number in the field, and is essential when preparing data to be read with the I specification.

The importance of this is shown by the example which follows.

Column number	**1 2 3 4 5**	**Value read using (I5)**
(a)	3 2	32000
(b)	3 2	3200
(c)	3 2	320
(d)	3 2	32

The field width is determined by the programmer when he designs the form of his data. It may be as small as 1, and the upper limit may be any convenient value. For output, it may be convenient to allow more space than is strictly needed to contain an integer (which will be output automatically right-adjusted) so as to get comfortable separation from the preceding number printed on the same line and thus improve the legibility of the printed information. It is important, when using the I specification for output, to make sure that the field width you allow is enough to contain all the digits of the largest number expected and also the sign of any which happen to be negative. If you fail to do this, the result will be *overflow* of your number (too big for the space allowed) and possible loss of the information.

Now let us examine our example again. The READ statement, when encountered during the execution of the program, will cause the computer to activate the card reader, in effect, and scan the next data card, or cards, in accordance with the instructions which it finds in the field specifications of the FORMAT statement referenced by the READ statement. The READ (or WRITE) and FORMAT statements do not need to be physically next to one another: the connection is established by the reference in the input or output statement. Since the FORMAT statement does not represent an executable instruction, it may be placed anywhere in the program and will be invoked only by an associated input/output statement. Some programmers, for easy reference, group all their FORMAT statements at the front or the end of the program. When only a single reference is made to it, however, it is usually most convenient to have the FORMAT statement next to its READ or WRITE statement. It is worth noting that any number of READs and WRITEs may refer to a single FORMAT statement. But we digress.

On meeting the READ statement, the system determines that it has to read a value from a card and assign it to the variable called MA. The list of specifications inside the parentheses of the FORMAT statement is now scanned, from left to right, and the I5 specification is found. This is interpreted as meaning that the required value will be found in the first five columns of the next data card, and that it should be treated as an integer. This value will now be read and assigned to the variable MA. Even if the field contains fewer than five characters, it will be read in correctly as long as they are right-adjusted within it.

Spacing

In the example considered above, it was assumed that the field—in this case, five characters wide—started in the first column of the data card (or *input record*). We should also think about how we might handle the situation if the data field were in, say, columns 11 to 15, with columns 1 to 10 of no interest.

What is needed is some means of telling the computer to skip over those first ten columns, looking only at the information which comes after this. This facility is provided by the 'X' field specification. The revised FORMAT statement would look like this:

```
    1 FORMAT(10X, I5)
```

which would be interpreted as: 'Skip (i.e. ignore) the first ten columns on the data card, and take the integer information required from the next five columns.' If it were wanted to skip twelve columns, the field specification would be 12X. Thirty-five columns could be skipped by specifying 35X, and so on. The character 'X'—a normal capital letter X—means that some part of the card is to be ignored, treated as though it were spaces, and the exact size of this skipped field is given by the number which precedes the X.

This field specification can be used for output as well, and here it is always interpreted as meaning 'Output the given number of spaces'. So the effect of:

```
    WRITE(3, 100), I, J, K
100 FORMAT (10X, I3, 12X, I4, 5X, I5)
```

is to print a line which looks like this:

ƀƀƀƀƀƀƀƀƀ*xxx*ƀƀƀƀƀƀƀƀƀƀƀƀ*xxxx*ƀƀƀƀƀ*xxxxx*

where ƀ again represents a space and *x* represents any constituent of an integer—digit, space or sign.

If you count the number of blank characters printed for the 10X specification, you will discover that there are only *nine* of them. What happened to the tenth? It will be found that 12X produces twelve spaces, and 5X causes five spaces to be printed. Only the first field has failed to come out correctly.

This is nothing to worry about, and is quite normal in Fortran systems. The information to be printed (and this applies only to *output* of data) is sent to the printer as a string of characters, which are collected together and formed into a line of print before the operation which finally produces the hard copy is executed. But one more item of information is needed by the printer before the hammers strike the ribbon and leave their impression on the paper: which line is it to be printed on? The next? Or the next but one? Or on a new page? Or some combination of these? This information is acquired by the printer by peeling off the very first character sent to it for output and interpreting it in a different way. It is *not* printed but is used to control the selection of the next line to be printed on, and is called the *carriage control* character. This explains why, earlier in this chapter, it was stated that only 119 characters per line were printed by a 120-character printer and only 131 by a 132-character machine. The first character sent out to build a line always gets lost, since it has a carriage control function.

In practice, there are only three carriage control characters worth bothering about. These are the characters '0' (zero), '1' (one) and 'b̸' (blank), which have the following effects *before* anything is printed:

Control character	**Effect on printer carriage**
0	Skip one line
blank	Move to the next line
1	Move to a new page

Some machines have a facility for printing on the same line as was used in the previous WRITE statement, using the control character '+', but this is rarely used. If it is available on your equipment, the Fortran manual will explain its use, which is often rather different from that of the other three characters.

To return to the X field specification, can you see anything wrong with the following FORMAT statement, used for input from a punched card?

```
100 FORMAT (77X, I5)
```

Well, of course! The number of characters specified altogether is too many for a punched card. Add 77 to 5 and the answer is 82, but there are only 80 columns on a card. At execution time, the machine should indicate an error. The statement would be quite valid used in conjunction with a

WRITE statement for a line printer, since at least 119 character positions (*print positions*) would be available.

Here is another example of a FORMAT statement controlling several variables. This time an input situation is used. It is required to read in, from punched cards, values for the four variables K, I, L and M. K and I can have at most three digits each, whereas L and M may have as many as four digits. The four numbers are held on a single card in the following way:

K occupies columns 34 to 37 inclusive
I occupies columns 40 to 43 inclusive
L occupies columns 45 to 49 inclusive
M occupies columns 60 to 64

Try to write an appropriate READ-FORMAT sequence, and compare it with the answer given below.

```
  READ(2, 2) K, I, L, M
2 FORMAT (33X, I4, 2X, I4, 1X, I5, 10X, I5)
```

Note the use of I4 to allow for the possibility of a negative three-digit number and of I5 to allow for a negative four-digit number.

The set of field specifications contained within the parentheses of the FORMAT statement is scanned from left to right, and when the right-hand parenthesis is encountered it implies that no further reading or printing is required on that card or line. If there is no more information to be transferred, the process of input or output will stop. If there still remains information to be transferred, a new line or card will be started and, in the simple cases which we have considered so far, the FORMAT statement will be *re-scanned* starting again at the left-hand field specification. Later, we shall see that this re-scanning process can be more complicated.

Just as the X specification enables spaces on a card to be skipped over, there is a facility for the skipping of whole lines or cards. Let us suppose that, in our previous example, K and I were on one card, and that L and M were on the next card in the deck. Fig. 6.1 shows the arrangement.

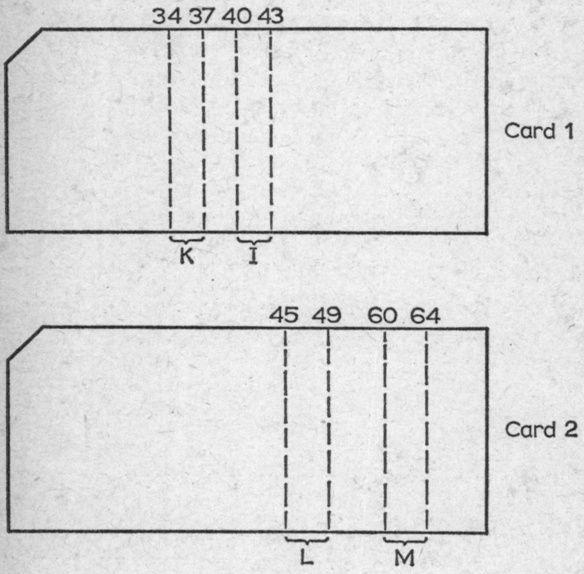

Fig. 6.1

We shall have to instruct the machine to read K and I from the first card, then ignore the rest of that card and skip to the next, from which L and M are to be read. There are a number of ways in which this might be done, but the most straightforward is to use the following sequence:

```
  READ(2, 1) K, I
1 FORMAT (33X, I4, 2X, I4)
  READ(2, 2) L, M
2 FORMAT (44X, I5, 10X, I5)
```

If you check this against Fig. 6.1, you will see that it should give the desired result. Alternatively, the same result could be achieved by using a single READ statement and the special symbol in the FORMAT statement which indicates 'end of unit record (card or line)'. This symbol is the slash '/'—the same symbol as is used for the division operator, but there is no possibility of confusion since the context in which it is used is entirely different. When this symbol is used, it replaces the comma which would have been used as a separator between adjacent field specifications. Our modified sequence could now be:

```
   READ (2, 10) K, I, L, M
10 FORMAT (33X, I4, 2X, I4 / 44X, I5, 10X, I5)
```

Notice that when a new unit record is started, the card is scanned from column 1 again. See how the slash replaces the comma which would otherwise have separated 'I4' and '44X'.

This feature can be used for output also, but here a little more care is needed. When a slash is used to indicate the end of a unit record (in this case, a line of output), the remainder of the information which is transferred will go to a new line. It follows that another control character will be needed to position the carriage correctly, and this character will be the first one transferred after the slash is dealt with. Here is an example, showing the output of K, I, L and M onto two lines, double-spaced, to make the principle quite clear:

```
    WRITE (3, 200) K, I, L, M
200 FORMAT (11X, I4, 5X, I4 / 10X, I5, 4X, I5)
```

The final tabulation should be:

b̸b̸b̸b̸b̸b̸b̸b̸b̸b̸*xxxx*b̸b̸b̸b̸b̸*xxxx*
b̸b̸b̸b̸b̸b̸b̸b̸b̸*xxxxx*b̸b̸b̸b̸*xxxxx*

The symbols used have the same meanings as before.

Multiple skipping

If it is desired to skip not just one line or card but several, more than one slash may be used. But the exact number used depends on whether they will appear in the middle of the set of format specifications or at one end. Different Fortran systems tend to differ here, but it usually happens that if *n* slashes appear at the beginning or end of a format list, then *n* unit records are skipped (*n* lines or *n* cards); if the *n* slashes appear in the middle of the list, then $n - 1$ unit records will be skipped. Thus, on input, the effect of the FORMAT:

```
FORMAT (I6 / / I4, I5)
```

is to read a value from the first card, skip the next card, then read two values from the third. The *two* slashes in the middle cause *one* card to be skipped. This is because the slash is an *end of unit record* indicator. The first slash indicates the end of information on the first card, the second slash indicates the end of information on the second card—even though none had been transferred off it into memory.

On output, the effect of the FORMAT:

```
FORMAT (I4, I5, I6 / / / )
```

would be to print three values on the next line, then skip *three* lines. This is because the final right parenthesis of the FORMAT statement also acts as an end of unit record indicator, so we have an effective *four* record terminators, causing *three* to be skipped.

This one:

```
FORMAT (/ / / 1X, I3, 2X, I7)
```

terminates *three* records—and so skips *three* lines—before output of two values on the next line. '1X' is here used for carriage control. As can be seen, no separators are needed between the slashes.

The 'H' field specification—Hollerith output

This field specification is very useful when it is required to print headings or any other textual information. Suppose that a program were being written to convert sterling amounts into dollars. We might very well need a heading such as:

CONVERSION TABLE

nicely centred in the page. This could be achieved by means of a WRITE statement with the appropriate FORMAT statement. No WRITE list will be needed, though we could have one if it were required to intersperse results with the text. Here is how it could be done:

```
  WRITE (3, 1)
1 FORMAT (52X, 16HCONVERSION TABLE)
```

The purpose of the 52X specification is to cause the output of fifty-two spaces at the beginning of a new line (the first space goes for carriage control). After this comes the specification starting '16H', which means: 'What follows the "H" is a string of sixteen alphabetic, numeric and special characters which are to be printed exactly as they appear here.'

The machine will then print each of the sixteen characters following the 'H', whatever they may be, starting with that character *immediately* following the 'H'. Any character of the Fortran character set may be used, and many systems allow extra, but useful, characters to be printed as well. If a blank space is found within the Hollerith field—that is, the field defined here by '16H'—a space will be printed. *This is the one instance in the Fortran language when spaces have any significance.*

The number preceding the 'H' must be exactly equal to the number of characters, including blanks, in the message to be output.

Here is another example to show how values and textual material may be output together. Two values are available for output. Their names are LENGTH and JANGLE. It is required that they should be printed on the same line, each preceded by its name, LENGTH in print positions 14 to 19 inclusive and JANGLE in print positions 31 to 35 inclusive. The following is one way of doing this:

```
          WRITE (3, 444) LENGTH, JANGLE
      444 FORMAT (5X, 9HLENGTHb̸=b̸, I6,
         *            2X, 9HJANGLEb̸=b̸, I5)
```

and the result would look like this (assuming LENGTH and JANGLE to have the values 23 and 47 respectively):

```
b̸b̸b̸b̸LENGTHb̸=b̸b̸b̸b̸b̸23b̸b̸JANGLEb̸=b̸b̸b̸b̸47
```

Or, more precisely, since the spaces do not print:

```
    LENGTH =     23  JANGLE =    47
```

Mr Hollerith was a pioneer of punched card processing, and the letter 'H' used in the field specification, being the first letter of his name, is our way of honouring him. A string of characters headed by '*n*H', where *n* is the number of characters in the string, is called a *Hollerith constant*. In standard Fortran, there is no such thing as a Hollerith *variable*.

The 'F' field specification

This is a way of specifying the layout of real numbers—those which are held in memory as floating-point quantities. When you want to print real numbers in their everyday representation, such as −27.346, this is the field specification to use.

The general form of this specification is:

F*w*.*d*

where *w* is the *total width* of the field containing the number, and *d* is the number of digits to be printed *after the decimal point*.

The phrase 'total width' is important. It includes all the digits of the number, both before and after the decimal point, and also an allowance of two character positions for the decimal point (which is *always* printed) and a possible negative sign. If the value is positive, no plus sign is output, but there will be a space where it would have been.

A little calculation will persuade the reader that *w* is always larger than *d* by at least 2. Some systems always print the '0' in front of the decimal point of numbers less than 1, and if this is the case the minimum difference between *w* and *d* becomes 3. Assuming this to be the case, it follows that there can be no meaningful output if the total field width allowed is less than three characters. If the field width exceeds the amount of space needed to contain a value, the value will be printed right-adjusted in the field, which will be left-filled with spaces.

Look at this typical F specification:

F9.3

This means that the required field width is nine print positions, and that there will be three digits printed after the decimal point. If the value being output has a fraction part too large to be accommodated in the space allowed, the value will be rounded to fit. If the whole-number part is too big for the space allowed, an overflow condition exists. If this happens, digits may be lost from the left-hand end of the number. The way in which this condition is signalled varies from machine to machine.

Here are several numbers output using the F9.3 specification:

0.0123456 is output as	ƀƀƀƀ0.012
0.1234567	ƀƀƀƀ0.123
1.2345678	ƀƀƀƀ1.235
12.345678	ƀƀƀ12.346
12345.678	12345.678
—234.5678	ƀ—234.568
—6.3	ƀƀƀ—6.300
—3456.789	—3456.789
—12345.678	Overflow—no room for the sign

The F specification may be used just as well for input as for output. The field width and number of decimal places may be specified exactly as explained above for output. But there is an important difference: the field width is always given the meaning described previously, but the number of decimal places is used *only if no decimal point is punched in the data field.* This is an economical measure, for it allows numbers to be punched without decimal points, and thus more numbers to be punched on a card. The exact position which the decimal point should occupy is defined by the *d* parameter of the format specification. For example, given the following data:

12345678901234567890

and this FORMAT statement:

```
FORMAT (F8.4, F6.2, F6.3)
```

if three real values are read from the card, they will be +1234.5678, +9012.34 and +567.890.

Many people, however, like their data to be more readable than this, so that it can be checked by eye. They will be relieved to know that the decimal point may be punched, and whatever the value of the *d* parameter the number of decimal places punched will override that value. So, given this data card:

```
123.456.789.0
```

and this FORMAT statement:

```
FORMAT (F7.4, F3.1, F3.0)
```

the values read will be +123.456, +0.78 and +9.0. The number of decimal places is that *actually punched* on the card.

Here is one last example. It is required to input the value of a variable A(M), which is expected to be less than 1000.0. The decimal point will be punched in the field, and the field itself begins at column 12 on the card. The value will never be negative, but there may be up to six places of decimals.

Since the value will always be positive or zero, there is no need to allow room for a sign. We shall need room for, at most, three digits in the whole number part, a decimal point, and six digits in the fraction part of the number—a total of ten characters. F10.6 should be a satisfactory field specification, then. But F10.0 would have been equally good, since the decimal point will always be there on the data card. We will also need to skip over the first eleven columns of the card, because the data field starts in column 12. The following should be all right:

```
   READ (2,45) A(M)
45 FORMAT (11X, F10.6)
```

The 'E' field specification

'E' is for exponential, and a number output using this field specification will be in exponential (i.e. floating-point) form. For input purposes, the 'E' specification may be taken to have the same effect as an 'F' specification having the same field width.

Numbers output in floating-point form will have the general appearance:

$$\pm.xxxxxx\mathrm{E}\pm yy$$

where *xxxxxx* are the digits of the mantissa (fraction part) of the number, and *yy* are the digits of the exponent (the power of 10 by which the mantissa is to be multiplied).

If the mantissa is negative, it will be preceded by a minus sign; if not, the plus sign will be suppressed and replaced by a space. The exponent is always signed, even when it is positive.

The general form of this specification is:

E*w*.*d*

where *w* is again the total field width and *d* is the number of digits wanted in the mantissa.

There are six spaces in any floating-point number which must be filled before we start thinking about the mantissa. These are: the sign of the mantissa, the decimal point, the letter 'E' which divides the mantissa from the exponent, the sign of the exponent and the two digits of the exponent itself. It follows that the minimum field width is seven characters, and that the difference between *w* and *d* must be at least six. Many beginning Fortran programmers forget this, and get strange-looking output as a result.

A typical number output in exponential form would look like this:

−.154376E+02

which represents the value −15.4376, of course, and might have been printed using the field specification E12.6 (twelve character positions altogether, six significant figures). Numbers punched in this notation can be read using an E field specification.

There is no reason why one should not read some real and some integer values from the same card, and some of the real values might be expressed in exponential form, others in a more conventional manner. It is reasonable, therefore, to expect to meet FORMAT statements in which all three field specifications occur. Something like this:

```
  READ (2, 3) JVC, DATE, EVEN
3 FORMAT (I5 / F10.3, 5X, E11.5)
```

This causes JVC to be read from the first five columns of the first card, as an integer, then DATE and EVEN are read from the next card, DATE in any of the accepted real forms and EVEN in exponential form. There is a five-column gap between the DATE and EVEN fields.

Multiple and repeated field specifications

Here is an interesting sequence:

```
  READ(2, 2) (DATA(K), K = 1, 20)
2 FORMAT (F9.3)
```

Does something seem a little wrong? You might well think so, for while the READ statement calls for the processing of twenty numbers, the FORMAT statement contains a field specification for one number only. But, in fact, all is well, and both statements are perfectly valid. What will happen is this.

K will be assigned the value 1, and DATA(1) will be read in, using the field specification F9.3. Now the Fortran system has a problem. It has reached the extreme right-hand parenthesis of the FORMAT statement, but there are still nineteen numbers left in the READ list (DATA(2) to DATA(20)). There is really only one thing to do, isn't there? The closing parenthesis is treated as an end of record indicator, and the set of field specifications is scanned backwards until an opening parenthesis is found. In this simple instance, there is only the one opening (i.e. left-hand) parenthesis, and when this is reached the direction of scan is reversed and input of values continues. Each scan of the field specification results in the input of one value, until the READ list is exhausted. In our example there will be twenty forward scans of the FORMAT list, and so twenty numbers will be read *from twenty cards.*

The re-scanning principle can be extended to the cases when there is more than one pair of parentheses in a FORMAT statement. The following is an example of such an arrangement:

```
34 FORMAT (F9.3, F9.3 / (F9.3))
                        *
```

When re-scanning is required, the point at which the re-scan starts is always either the left-most opening parenthesis or, if there are more than one pair, the opening parenthesis corresponding to the last-but-one closing parenthesis. In our example, this is the one marked with an asterisk beneath it. However, a little caution is needed when using this feature, and the exact working for the system you are using should be checked with the system Fortran manual.

If, now, we execute the statement:

```
READ (2, 34) A, B, (BETA(J), J = 1, 15)
```

then A and B will be read from the first card, and the fifteen elements of the array BETA will be taken one from each of the next fifteen cards. This is because the re-scanning process is 'looping' on that final (F9.3) specification. It will continue to do this until all the items of the READ list have been used up, and then the next statement will be executed.

Balanced parentheses are just as important in a FORMAT statement as they are anywhere else in a Fortran program. The number of closing parentheses must be exactly equal to the number of opening parentheses.

When a field specification, or a set of field specifications, is repeated, we can save ourselves some writing effort by making use of *repetition factors*. Take the example used above as an instance: instead of writing F9.3 twice in the early part of the statement we could just as well have written 2F9.3. This would alter the FORMAT statement to:

```
34 FORMAT (2F9.3 / (F9.3))
```

Such use of repetition is very convenient and often found. Of course, if A and B had different field specifications, no abbreviation would be possible.

Other input/output devices

In the READ and WRITE statements which have been seen so far, the peripheral code '2' has been used for the card reader and the code '3' has represented the line printer. It has already been pointed out that other codes can be allocated to other devices, such as a teletype, card punch, paper tape reader or punch, and so on. The set of codes used will depend on the equipment available in the computer installation, and on the compiler which is in use. Although the codes in the READ and WRITE statements have, so far, invariably been integer constants, it is permitted that they may be integer variables if this is convenient. Thus we might have a statement such as:

```
READ (INPUT, 3) A, B, C
```

which means: 'Read the values for the variables A, B and C from whatever peripheral device has the code corresponding to the current value of the variable INPUT; the transfer is to be controlled by the FORMAT statement numbered 3.'

At some earlier point in the program, the statement:

```
INPUT = 2
```

might have appeared, and so the READ statement would be equivalent to:

```
READ (2, 3) A, B, C
```

This facility, which applies in exactly the same way to the WRITE statement, allows programs to be transferred from one computer to another, having different peripheral device codes, very often simply by changing one or two statements (those setting the values of INPUT, and other device variables) rather than changing every READ and WRITE statement.

Magnetic tape

Data may be recorded on magnetic tape in much the same way as music and speech, and later it may be 'played back' into main memory. The process of recording is called *writing*, and the playback is called *reading*. Both of these can be accomplished by using the READ and WRITE statements already described, with the appropriate peripheral code, i.e. that for the magnetic tape unit being used. To be sure of locating the recorded information when it is read back, it is usual to start recording from some fixed reference point. This is usually the beginning of the tape, and this position is reached by issuing a command to *rewind* the tape:

```
REWIND 5
```

will have the effect of rewinding the tape unit designated '5'. Only one tape unit may be specified in each REWIND statement.

When as much information has been recorded as is required, it is usual to mark its end by a specially recorded *file mark* immediately following the last record on the tape. This can be achieved by the command:

```
ENDFILE 5
```

which will place a file mark at the current writing position on tape unit 5. Again, not more than one tape unit may be specified in an ENDFILE statement.

Unformatted input and output

One of the main uses of magnetic tape is for the storage of intermediate results—not the final answers, but information which will be referred to again at some later stage of the calculation.

When this is the case, there is little point in devising a careful layout, for the results will never be printed. All that needs to be known is the order in which the information is held on tape, so that it can be properly recovered later. Consequently, no reference to a FORMAT statement is necessary, and the input and output statements for such *binary* information transfer have the general form:

READ (*dev*) *list of variables*
or WRITE (*dev*) *list of variables*

in which *dev* represents the device code of the tape unit in use.

When reading a record, it is important that the READ list should have the same number and type of variables as the corresponding WRITE.

Finally, a record is written to tape by each WRITE statement. After this has been done, it is possible to reposition the tape at the beginning of the record just written by the statement:

BACKSPACE *dev*

It is dangerous to attempt to write a record between two other records by the use of multiple BACKSPACEs. Because of minute fluctuations in tape movement speeds, there is always the possibility that the new record takes more space than the old, and it may overlap the next.

Alphanumeric data—the 'A' field specification

To round off this chapter, let us briefly examine one other type of specification which is rather different from those which have been considered up to now. This is the 'A' field specification for alphanumeric information.

Sometimes we shall want to read in textual information rather than numeric data. An example which springs to mind is the names of the workers on a firm's payroll, which will eventually be printed out together with the results of the calculations which have been carried out. What we do is to consider that each printable character is represented internally by a numeric code, and that this coding of characters into numbers is performed automatically by the computer.

The information is usually stored in memory cells which are identified by being given variable names. Each cell will be able to hold a certain maximum number of coded characters. What that number is will vary from machine to machine, and it may even be different for integer and real variables in the same machine. For the sake of example, it will be assumed in what follows that both real and integer variables are capable of holding five characters, but this is another point on which those with access to a computer should check with the system manual.

Let us suppose that the first ten columns on a data card contain a message (it could be a name—JANEbCLARK, for instance), and that we wish to store this name, just as if it were a number, inside the machine. We could use the following sequence of statements:

```
    READ (2, 1) NAME(1), NAME(2)
  1 FORMAT (2A5)
```

The FORMAT statement specifies that, on each card (only one in this case), there will be two (2) alphanumeric (A) fields, each one being five (5) character positions wide—2A5. So the first five characters on the card will be encoded into numerical form and assigned to the variable NAME(1). The next five will be similarly assigned to NAME(2). The information has here been read into an array, NAME, and this is often done to keep a string of characters together in one place under one name. But it is not strictly necessary to do it this way, and we could just as well have read in two unrelated variables, thus:

```
      READ (2, 1) D, B
```

The next problem is to convert the values held in the variables, whether simple or subscripted, back into alphanumeric form for printing. In fact, it is a very easy matter: we simply use a WRITE statement in conjunction with another 'A' field specification:

```
      WRITE (3,25) NAME(1), NAME(2)
   25 FORMAT (10X, 2A5)
```

The '10X' is used to give some initial spacing on the line.

The general form of the 'A' specification is:

*n*A*x*

where *n* is the repetition factor, and may be omitted, and *x* is the number of characters which can be contained in a memory cell, at most, *or some value less than that.*

There is no need to pack the maximum possible number of characters into a variable if it would be more convenient to pack in fewer of them. The information can be packed one character per memory word if you feel like it, and this is sometimes done when it is required to make textual changes after the data have been read in, as in a program to perform an editing function. The important thing is that, if the output is to match the input, the field specification used for output should be exactly the same as that used for input.

Exercises

1. Some of the following statements are incorrect, while others are quite valid. Select those which are wrong, and

give your reasons. Assume the card reader and line printer to be devices 2 and 3 respectively.

```
(a) READ (2, 35) A, TH(9)
(b) READ (2, 67) MAR
(c) READ (3, 56) X(I), K
(d) WRITE (3, 89) J K L M
(e) READ,(2, 87) V
(f) WRITE (3, −65) CXQ(7)
(g) WRITE(3,45) −H(7),RAD,−T
(h) READ (2, 296) (R(K), K = 1, 89)
(i) READ (3, 999, RESULT(J), J = 1, 10)
(j) READ (2, 2) P(2*I−J)
```

2. An array called TURN, which has thirty rows and four columns, is to be read in row by row (i.e. TURN(1, 1) then TURN(1, 2), and so on). The values are held on data cards, two per card, close-spaced and starting in column 1, and each is specified by F9.4. Write a suitable sequence of statements for the input of the array.

3. Determine which of the following FORMAT statements are invalid, and give your reasons:

```
(a)       FORMAT (F9.6)
(b)     3 FORMAT (12X, 2F9.12)
(c)    56 FORMAT (10X, E12.6 / 12X, F9.2)
(d)    60 FORMAT (///////)
(e)   986 FORMAT (20E12.6)
(f)     5 FORMAT (5X, 5HRESULTS)
(g)     8 FORMAT (3X, 3F8.2 / (F7.1)
(h)    10 FORMAT (7A4)
(i)   351 FORMAT F9.3)
(j)     1 FORMAT (4X, I7, 5X,I5 // F9.9)
```

4. The results from a certain program are to be printed on a line printer. At their head, in the approximate centre of the line, the following message must be printed:

   UPDATED STOCK RECORD

   Then two lines are to be skipped and on the next line, also centred, the message:

   CITY BRANCH

   is to appear. Write a suitable sequence of statements to perform this operation.

5. Answer question 2 again, but this time read the array in column by column order.

6. Three variables, SUM, DIFF and LIM, are to have their values both printed out and punched into cards. SUM and DIFF are to have two places of decimals, and may range in value from −999.99 to +9999.99. The range for LIM is from −9999 to +99999. Five spaces are to be left in front of each number, and all three are to be printed on one line and punched on a single card. Assuming that the device code for the card punch is 4, write a sequence of statements to perform the desired operations.

7. Repeat question 6, except that each number should be printed on a new line and punched on a new card.

8. The first twenty columns of a data card can contain alphabetic information which has to be read into the computer. Assuming that the first few elements of a one-dimensioned array called ALPHA are to be used to store this information, write a suitable sequence of instructions.

9. Say whether each of the following statements is true or false:

   (*a*) All the print positions of a 120-column line printer are available for printing.
   (*b*) Every READ and WRITE statement must have its own FORMAT statement.
   (*c*) All FORMAT statements must be labelled.
   (*d*) A FORMAT statement must always be physically the next statement in a program following the WRITE statement.
   (*e*) A READ statement may have an empty list.
   (*f*) It is not permitted to mix real and integer variables in the same READ or WRITE list.
   (*g*) If an entire array is to be read in by specifying only the array name, then it will be processed in column-wise manner.
   (*h*) The output field specification F9.2 implies that the number in question has seven digits of which two come after the decimal point.

7 Programs

The Fortran features with which we have dealt so far should enable us to write useful programs for the solution of a very wide variety of problems. It is true that there are a number of points which we have not yet touched upon, but these will be mentioned—where they are of importance to the beginning programmer—later in this and the succeeding chapters. For the moment, however, let us try writing one or two programs, putting into practice some of the theory which we have learnt.

To start with, consider the following problem, in which we assume that there is a relationship between the quantities V and I given by the following formula:

$$I = aV + bV^2 + cV^3$$

a, *b* and *c* are *coefficients* of unknown value. The problem is to produce results which will enable us to draw a graph relating I and V. The program should be sufficiently general that we can alter the values of the coefficients, and deal with several ranges of V and I. The approach will be to allow V to take a series of values, with the coefficients fixed, and calculate the value of I corresponding to each V value, using the formula given above.

The first thing to do is to make sure that we understand the problem. This having been done, when the problem is not a trivial one, it is usually a great help to draw a flowchart. Fig. 7.1 is a flowchart for the solution of this particular problem, and will be seen to contain several

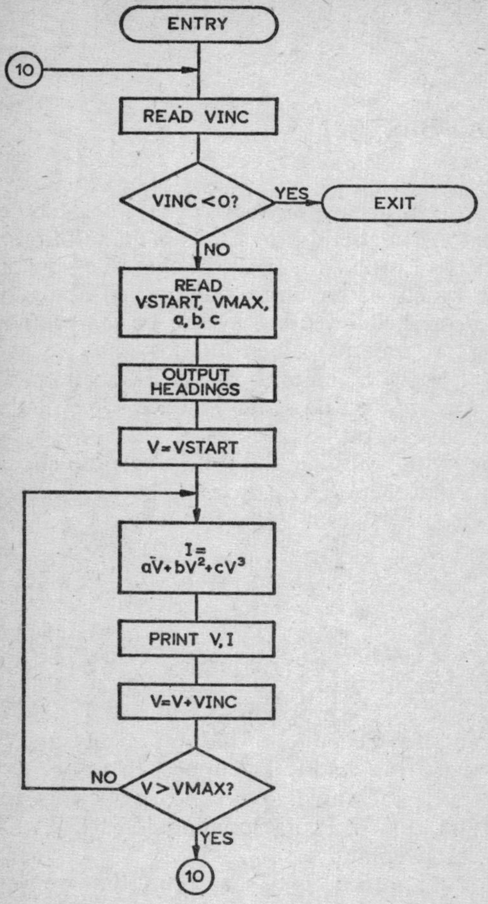
ENTRY
10
READ VINC
VINC < O?
YES
EXIT
NO
READ
VSTART, VMAX,
a, b, c
OUTPUT
HEADINGS
V=VSTART
I=
aV+bV²+cV³
PRINT V, I
V=V+VINC
NO
V > VMAX?
YES
10

Fig. 7.1

variable names which should be defined before we go any further.

a, *b* and *c*—coefficients;
VSTART—initial value of V;
VINC —V increment;
VMAX —maximum value of V, for a given set of coefficients, for which a value of I is to be calculated.

We start with an initial value for V called VSTART, and use this value in our formula to calculate the corresponding value for I. The value of V is then increased by the predetermined amount VINC, and the computation is repeated. This is done until the value of V exceeds some fixed value VMAX. The values of VINC, VSTART and VMAX will be read in at the start of the program, and after each calculation the values of V and I will be printed out. The final result will be a table which we can use as the data from which to draw our graph. The process will be repeated for different sets of data until an 'end-of-data' signal is encountered in the data. For our purpose, this signal will be a negative value for VINC—an abnormal value.

The first program action is the input of the value for VINC, which is immediately tested, to check whether it is the end-of-data signal, before values of VSTART, VMAX and the three coefficients A, B and C are read in.

Let us suppose that the three coefficients are all punched on one card, each in a ten-column field, and that the decimal points are punched. A suitable field specification for each of these would be F10.0, because the *d* parameter of the specification is redundant in the presence of a decimal point in the data. We shall suppose also that the real variables VSTART, VMAX and VINC are punched on separate cards, and that the same field specification is suitable for them.

The program so far, then, will be:

```
      READ (2, 100) VINC
  100 FORMAT (F10.0)
      IF (VINC .LT. 0.0) GO TO 99
      READ (2, 200) VSTART, VMAX, A, B, C
  200 FORMAT (F10.0/F10.0/3F10.0)
      . . .
```

Label 99 will be used to identify the exit point from the program. Study the READ statements and their associated FORMAT statements, and be sure that you understand them. If not, revise the relevant sections of Chapter 6.

Now the headings have to be printed at the top of the page. Something like this might be suitable:

```
        VOLTAGE               CURRENT
           V                     I
```

Try writing suitable WRITE and FORMAT statements. Remember to centre the headings nicely. Here is what the sequence so far should look like (the continuation, made necessary by the restricted page size of this book, may occur at a different point in practice, but this will not matter):

```
      READ (2, 100) VINC
  100 FORMAT (F10.0)
      IF (VINC .LT. 0.0) GO TO 99
      READ (2, 200) VSTART, VMAX, A, B, C
  200 FORMAT (F10.0/F10.0/3F10.0)
      WRITE (3, 300)
  300 FORMAT (1H1,  52X, 7HVOLTAGE,
     *               4X, 7HCURRENT,
     *              56X, 1HV, 10X, 1HI)
      . . .
```

There are several points of interest here. Notice the field specification '1H1' at the beginning of the FORMAT statement. This is a Hollerith constant, and its being in this position has the effect that the first character to reach the line printer is a '1'. This will be interpreted as a carriage control character and will cause the paper to be spaced to the top of the next page, or *head of form* (HOF) as it is frequently called. The WRITE statement associated with this FORMAT has no variable list, because no stored values are to be printed. And the continuation feature has been used, with an asterisk in column 6 to denote the continuation card.

These preliminaries completed, we can proceed to the calculation proper. The main formula evaluation has to be repeated until the value of VMAX is reached, increasing the value of V by VINC each time round the loop. The starting value of V must be VSTART. Also, the values of V and I will be printed out during each cycle.

A DO loop will not be used, though it could be if we were to count the loops instead of testing for a final value explicitly. This is shown later. So the main part of the program will start like this:

```
      V = VSTART
   10 CONTINUE
      XI = A * V + B * V ** 2 + C * V ** 3
      . . .
```

'XI' is used in lieu of 'I' to conform with the naming rules for real variables.

On each *cycle* (loop), the values of V and I must be printed. We must arrange the output so that the values of each come out under the appropriate heading. Suppose we want the results expressed in the conventional manner, and with two places of decimals. The page will look something like this:

VOLTAGE	CURRENT
V	I
1.50	7.13
2.50	24.38
3.50	63.13
4.50	410.09
etc.	etc.

A suitable field specification for the values would probably be F7.2, and we have to remember to insert spacing specifications to ensure that the figures are centred under their respective headings. Can you now produce the most suitable WRITE and FORMAT statements? When you have tried, have a look at the suggested solution below:

```
    WRITE (3, 400) V, XI
400 FORMAT (53X, F7.2, 4X, F7.2)
    . . .
```

All that remains is to increment V and, when the loop is completed, stop the execution of the program.

The STOP statement

The effect of this statement is to terminate the program currently executing.

It has the general form:

STOP

or, possibly,

STOP *n*

where *n* is a string of digits, none of which exceeds 7 (*octal digits*). Thus, if a program is written to have several exit points, they can be given different identification numbers, so that one may know exactly at what point execution was terminated, since the number is displayed at the operator's console when the program stops.

Execution is finished when a STOP statement is encountered, but it is possible to introduce a *pause* into a program. When this is done, the program is halted for the operator to take some essential action—such as mounting the correct magnetic tape on a suitable peripheral unit. When this has been done, the operator can issue a command from his console which will restart the program at the statement immediately following that which produced the pause. The statement used is:

PAUSE

or

PAUSE *n*

where *n* is again a string of octal digits. For both the STOP and PAUSE statements, the maximum size of the associated octal number is 77777.

The END statement

In every Fortran program, this is one statement which *must* appear. It is non-executable but essential, since it indicates to the compiler the physical end of the program. It should not be confused with the STOP statement, which may appear at any point in the program, and is executed when it is encountered. It takes the form

END

and starts in, or beyond, column 7.

We can now put everything together to form a complete Fortran program.

```
    5 READ (2, 100) VINC
  100 FORMAT (F10.0)
      IF (VINC .LT. 0.0) GO TO 99
      READ (2, 200) VSTART, VMAX, A, B, C
  200 FORMAT (F10.0/F10.0/3F10.0)
      WRITE (3, 300)
  300 FORMAT (1H1, 52X, 7HVOLTAGE,
     *              4X, 7HCURRENT,
     *             56X, 1HV, 10X, 1HI)
      V = VSTART
   10 XI = A*V + B*V**2 + C*V**3
      WRITE (3, 400) V, XI
  400 FORMAT (53X, F7.2, 4X, F7.2)
      V = V + VINC
      IF (V .GT. VMAX) GO TO 5
      GO TO 10
   99 STOP
      END
```

Increasing the value of a variable using a real increment, as shown here, may (because of the nature of the floating-point arithmetic processes) have the effect of introducing an error of steadily increasing magnitude. This can be minimised by using a multiplicative rather than an additive process, in a DO loop, but we shall need to compute the number of cycles, allowing for rounding errors, thus:

$$N = \left\lfloor \frac{\text{VMAX} + \text{VINC} - \text{VSTART}}{\text{VINC}} + 0.5 \right\rfloor$$

where ⌊. . .⌋ means 'the largest integer value not exceeding . . .'.

Our loop now becomes:

```
      . . .
      N = ((VMAX + VINC - VSTART)/VINC)
              + 0.5
```

```
      V = VSTART
      DO 10 J = 1, N
         XI = A*V + B*V**2 + C*V**3
         WRITE (3, 400) V, XI
400      FORMAT (. . .)
         XJ = J
         V = VSTART + XJ*VINC
   10 CONTINUE
      GO TO 5
   99 STOP
      END
```

It is worth noting that, on most systems, the statement:

```
CALL EXIT
```

is synonymous with STOP. Indeed it is preferred by some, since it transfers control to the operating system, whereas STOP may, literally, stop the computer completely, wasting valuable central processor time.

An insurance problem

An insurance company wishes to determine some statistics of the people whose lives it insures. Among other things, it is required to know:

1. The average age of all those insured.
2. The average sum for which each is insured.
3. The percentage of the total number of insured who are over 60 years of age.

Let us assume that there are N people holding life policies with our company and that, for each one, we have two pieces of information. The first is the age of the insured and the second is the amount for which insurance has been effected.

Before proceeding any further, it is suggested that you

draw a flowchart, determine the layout of data and output, and attempt to write a complete program to provide the information wanted by the company. Don't forget that headings will be needed.

Fig. 7.2 is a flowchart for a solution to this problem, and the program developed from it will be discussed here.

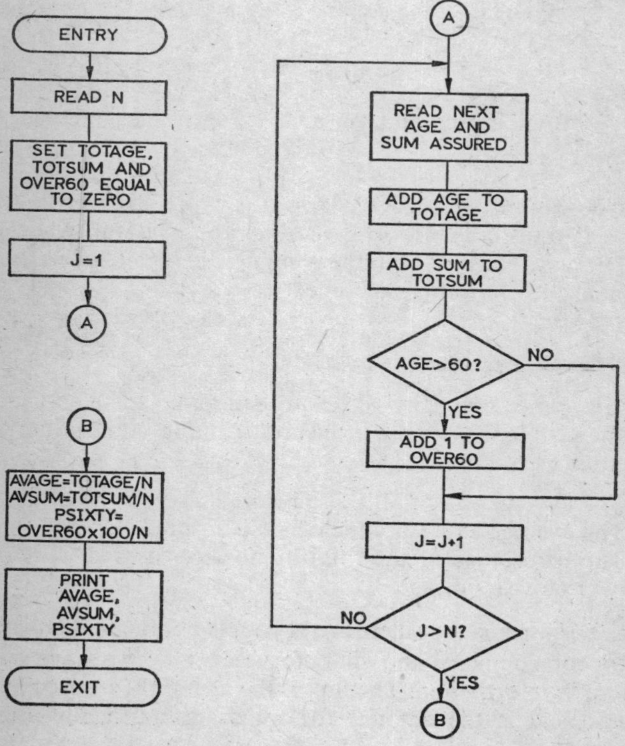

Fig. 7.2

To find the average age and sum assured, it is necessary to add together the ages and individual sums assured and divide each sum by N. This can be achieved during the process of reading the data, which need not be held permanently in high-speed memory. At the same time, each age is examined and compared with 60. When a value exceeding 60 is found, a counter is incremented. We thus get a count of the number of people over 60, and this can be expressed as a percentage, since we know the total number of those assured.

The following is a program which will produce the results which are wanted:

```
C *** INSURANCE PROBLEM
C
      READ (2, 100) N
  100 FORMAT (I6)
C *** INITIALISE SUMS
      TOTAGE = 0.0
      TOTSUM = 0.0
      OVER60 = 0.0
C *** MAIN LOOP
      DO 10 J = 1, N
C *** READ NEXT DETAIL CARD
      READ (2, 200) IAGE, SUM
  200 FORMAT (I2, 2X, F8.0)
C *** FLOAT INSURED'S AGE TO SIMPLIFY
C        ARITHMETIC
      AGE = IAGE
      TOTAGE = TOTAGE + AGE
C *** DEVELOPING SUMS FOR FINAL
C        AVERAGE
      TOTSUM = TOTSUM + SUM
      IF (IAGE .GT. 60) OVER60 = OVER60 + 1.0
   10 CONTINUE
C *** END OF LOOP
```

```
C *** WE NEED N IN FLOATING-POINT
C       FORM
      EN = N
C *** COMPUTE AVERAGES
      AVAGE = TOTAGE/EN
      AVSUM = TOTSUM/EN
C *** AND THE PERCENTAGE
      PSIXTY = (OVER60 * 100.0) / EN
C *** OUTPUT OF RESULTS
      WRITE(3, 300) AVAGE, AVSUM, PSIXTY
  300 FORMAT (51X,
     * 20HINSURANCE STATISTICS /
     * 15H0AVERAGE AGE IS, F4.1 /
     * 15H AVERAGE SUM IS, F12.2 /
     * 25H PERCENTAGE OVER SIXTY IS, F6.2)
      CALL EXIT
      END
```

TOTAGE represents the sum of the ages of the people insured;
TOTSUM is the total sum assured;
OVER60 is the number of people over 60 years of age;
PSIXTY is the percentage of the total who are over 60;
AGE and IAGE have the same value, but in real and integer form, respectively. The integer form is most likely to appear in the records, but the real form is needed for calculation.
EN is, similarly, the real form of N;
AVAGE is the average age of the customers;
AVSUM is the average sum assured.

Examine the program carefully, statement by statement, until you are sure of exactly what is happening. First a value of N is read from a card. The field specification is I6, which allows for up to 999999 customer records. Next, the variables TOTAGE, TOTSUM and OVER60 are initialised at a value of zero. This is a very important step: these variables are used to develop the final totals, and it may not be assumed that they have any specific value when first used—even zero. The initialisation completed, the DO loop is entered for the calculation of sums. On each cycle, data on a new person are input, and the person's age and sum assured are added to the accumulated sums so far. In addition, every age is checked against 60; this is the purpose of the IF statement. Ages greater than 60 cause the counter variable OVER60 to be incremented by 1, so that, when all the customer records have been processed, the value of OVER60 will equal the number of customers who are 60 or more years of age.

It remains now to compute the average age (AVAGE) and the average sum assured (AVSUM), which is done by dividing TOTAGE and TOTSUM respectively by the number of customers, N. Here a new problem arises. It is not permissible to divide directly by N, for this would involve us in mixed-mode arithmetic:

```
AVAGE = TOTAGE / N
```

for TOTAGE and TOTSUM are real variables, whereas N is of integer type. So a real value for N has to be computed, and this is done by writing:

```
EN = N
```

The same process was used to obtain a real value from IAGE earlier in the program:

```
AGE = IAGE
```

The statement involving PSIXTY converts the *number* of people over the age of 60 to a *percentage* of the total.

When all the calculations have been performed, the results are printed under suitable headings, and with appropriate identification. Note the use of continuation cards. Comments have been freely used throughout to help clarify the program. The first comment is useful in identifying the program deck. The blank comment after it is for emphasis of the title.

Disk storage

Earlier in this book it was stated that many modern computers are equipped with magnetic disk backing stores. Such stores typically consist of a set of flat disks, coated with a ferromagnetic material, rotated at high speed. Magnetic read and write heads are made to move across these disks to rigidly defined *tracks*. There are often 200 tracks per disk, and a great deal of data can be stored indefinitely. A typical disk storage unit (IBM model 3340) is shown in the photograph in Fig. 7.3.

Many Fortran compilers have statements for the control of data transfer to or from disk storage devices (often known as *mass storage*, because of their high data capacity), for these devices become very valuable when the amount of data to be processed is too great to fit into the immediate access (main) memory of the machine. Access to information on disk is much faster than to that on tape or cards, and so the facility is very valuable in such circumstances.

Each track on a disk is divided into a number of *records*, and each record contains a number of characters of data. Characters may be grouped into *words* of a size convenient to fit into a Fortran variable, but the actual word size depends on the physical characteristics of the computer being used.

The number of words constituting a record can often be selected by the user. Groups of records make up data *files*, and the number of such groups in a file is under programmer control. To review: data are held on disk in *files*, each file contains a number of *records*, and each record contains a number of *characters*.

There is no Fortran standard, at the time of writing

Fig. 7.3 (*Reproduced by courtesy of IBM United Kingdom Limited*)

(1974), which indicates the exact form that input–output statements for disk storage should take, and so it is not possible to give a detailed description of such statements here. Individual manufacturers have tended to make their own specifications to suit the equipment supplied with their computers, and the way in which the data is organised on such equipment. There are basic differences between, for instance, magnetic tape and magnetic disk which make the standard READ and WRITE statements not entirely suited to disk control. Interested readers should refer to the Fortran manual of the machine which they intend to use.

The EQUIVALENCE statement

It has been assumed so far that every storage location used was associated with a single variable name. But there are occasions when it is useful to be able to refer to such a location by two, or even more, variable names. If, for instance, a program refers to two different variables, A and B, but these two variables are never in active use at the same time, it would seem reasonable to allow them to share the same space in memory. This can be achieved by using the EQUIVALENCE statement:

EQUIVALENCE (A, B)

which states that both A and B are to share the same storage. They are said to have been *equivalenced* to one another—referring to A is equivalent to referring to B.

The general form of an EQUIVALENCE statement is:

EQUIVALENCE ($list_1$), ($list_2$), . . ., ($list_n$)

in which each *list* is of the form v_1, v_2, . . ., v_m and the *v*'s are either variables or the names of array elements. Each of the variables in a given list is equivalenced to all the others in the same list.

Another example of the use of EQUIVALENCE involves

arrays. Since arrays are stored sequentially in memory, it follows that the equivalencing of one element from each array has the effect of equivalencing a number of, or even all, the arrays' elements. Suppose that there exists a 2 × 5 array called ABLE. Under normal circumstances, the only way to refer to an element of the array would involve the use of two subscripts: we would speak of ABLE (1, 3) or ABLE (2, 2), for instance. Now let us introduce another array called BAKER, a one-dimensional array having ten elements. At this stage, we should recall the order in which the elements of ABLE and BAKER are held in memory. If they were held in memory cells 1001 to 1010, the relationship between element and location address would be as shown below:

1001	ABLE (1, 1)	BAKER (1)
1002	ABLE (2, 1)	BAKER (2)
1003	ABLE (1, 2)	BAKER (3)
1004	ABLE (2, 2)	BAKER (4)
1005	ABLE (1, 3)	BAKER (5)
1006	ABLE (2, 3)	BAKER (6)
1007	ABLE (1, 4)	BAKER (7)
1008	ABLE (2, 4)	BAKER (8)
1009	ABLE (1, 5)	BAKER (9)
1010	ABLE (2, 5)	BAKER (10)

Now, what happens if the statement:

```
EQUIVALENCE (ABLE (1, 1), BAKER (1))
```

appears in a program?

It specifies that the memory cell which contains the value called ABLE (1, 1) may also be referred to as BAKER (1). That is all! It does *not* suggest that location 1001 (in this case) could contain two different values at the same time. However, the effect is rather more wide-reaching than is immediately apparent. Because the arrays are stored in the way shown previously, it follows that when one element from each appears in an equivalencing operation the other elements are also affected, since storage is essentially sequential. So if ABLE (1, 1) is the same as BAKER (1), then ABLE (1, 4) will be the same as BAKER (7), and the content of location 1003 may be called either ABLE (1, 2) or BAKER (3).

This feature can often be quite useful when storage is at a premium and two arrays appear at mutually exclusive points in a program. Or a large routine may have been written by a team, and different people could have called the same variable by different names, due to poor initial planning. An equivalence operation in such circumstances can save an awful lot of error-prone changes. Sometimes it is used purely to improve the speed of operation. Suppose it is required to clear the whole array ABLE so that it contains only zeros. Here are two ways of doing this:

1.
```
      DIMENSION ABLE (2, 5)
      DO 10 I = 1, 2
      DO 5 J = 1, 5
         ABLE (I, J) = 0.0
    5 CONTINUE
   10 CONTINUE
      next statement
```

2.
```
      DIMENSION ABLE (2, 5), BAKER( 10)
      EQUIVALENCE (ABLE (1, 1), BAKER (1))
      DO 10 I = 1, 10
         BAKER (I) = 0.0
   10 CONTINUE
      next statement
```

The second is faster in its operation. If you write out the equivalent routines using IF statements, you will see why.

Incidentally, the order of variables in an EQUIVALENCE list is unimportant,

```
EQUIVALENCE (BAKER (1), ABLE (1, 1))
```

would be just as effective. The DIMENSION statement is still needed for arrays, of course.

There is no reason, in general, why real and integer variables should not be equivalenced, though a little care is needed. Also, some computers have *variable word-length*—that is, the amount of memory space used for a real variable may differ from that used for an integer. The Honeywell 200 series is an example of such a machine, and many modern mini-computers may have different storage requirements for different types of variable. If this is so, equivalencing real to integer may not work in the way the programmer intends it to, so it is probably best to avoid doing this unless one is sure that the word-lengths are the same.

An EQUIVALENCE statement can, in principle, be placed anywhere in the program. Many systems, however, insist that all specification statements—DIMENSION, EQUIVALENCE and one or two others which will be mentioned later—must precede all executable statements and, to avoid confusion, this is not a bad rule to adopt in any case.

Exercises

1. The results of a medical survey of the growth of 400 children are held on punched cards. Each card contains the following information, in the order stated, punched (with decimal points) in seven columns with no spaces left between the numbers:

   age in years
   height in cm
   weight in kg

Write a complete program, including the necessary input and output statements and suitable comments, to determine:

(*a*) the average height of those children in the sample aged between 5 and 7 years;
(*b*) the number of children in the sample over 7 years of age;
(*c*) the average weight of all the children over 125 cm tall.

2. Write a program which will determine the smallest of a group of positive numbers, all less than 100, and print it out, together with a suitable message. No two numbers in the group will be the same. The numbers are punched on cards, five to a card, in fields twelve columns wide separated by four spaces. The very first card contains, in its first three columns, an integer value which is the number of numbers on the cards which follow. These latter are in real form.

(*Hint:* Make a note of the first number, and then compare the second number with it. If the second number is smaller, use it to replace the reference value. Repeat with the third, fourth, etc. numbers until the data are exhausted. The smallest will now be in the reference position.)

3. Write a program to print, under the headings:

X   X SQUARED

a table of squares of integers from 1 to 150 in steps of 1. The numbers should be printed, double-spaced, twenty-five to a page. The headings must be repeated on every page, and the pages should be numbered.

4. A real, one-dimensional array, XVAL, has forty-five elements. Both real and integer variables occupy the same amount of memory space. Each element of XVAL is to be

converted to integer form and stored in an array IVAL of the same size and dimensionality as XVAL. After this, there will be no further reference to XVAL, and IVAL has not been referenced previously in the program. Write an economical Fortran program segment to perform the required operation.

5. Correct the following EQUIVALENCE statements:

   (*a*) EQUIVALENCE,(A,G,DRAW)
   (*b*) EQUIVALENCE F, T, B, VOTE

8 Functions and subroutines

The piece of program between its first statement and the END statement which should be its last is called a *program unit*. There are a number of different kinds of program unit, and that with which we have dealt so far is known as a *main program*.

Right at the start of the book, the development of computers over the past twenty-five years or so was briefly discussed. In particular, mention was made of the developments and improvements which have produced high-level programming languages, of which Fortran is an example. You may recall that, in the early days of programming, each operation had to be programmed individually, and that a feature which we now take more or less for granted—such as division—required complex sequences of machine language instructions. Later, the autocodes made their appearance, and such sequences were now able to be expressed by a single code word or symbol. What had happened was that someone had realised that all divisions (or whatever the process might be) are very much the same, and that if the basic set of machine instructions is stored away somewhere in the machine it can be recovered and inserted into a program when a trigger word, such as 'DIV', appears in the source program. Alternatively, to save program instruction space, a branch to the stored routine could be inserted into the program at that point, and a return made to the main program when the work had been done. Such sets of instructions for general use were called *subroutines*, and they are widely used in all programming systems, including Fortran, today. In Fortran, we speak of program units called *subprograms*, which are separately compiled, but subordinate, program units designed to do specific jobs when called upon to do so by the main program. The two main types of subprogram are the *function subprogram* and the *subroutine subprogram*. We shall deal first with the function subprogram (or, simply, *function*), of which there are several types.

External library functions

The square root extraction is an arithmetic operation which is needed fairly regularly. Let us suppose that we are writing a program to print a table of numbers and their square roots. There are a number of complicated algorithms we could adopt, but Fortran affords the user a very much simpler solution. If the number whose square root is required is held in the variable X, all we have to do is to write:

```
Y = SQRT (X)
```

and the value of the square root of X will be assigned to the variable Y. 'SQRT' is a form of code word which says to the computer: 'Now calculate the square root of the number called X. Specific instructions for doing this are held in your program library in a small program called SQRT.'

You will gather from this that, as well as the compilers it needs, and the supervisory program (if any), the computer has stored a *library* of useful programs (actually subprograms) which can be called upon to perform useful mathematical calculations in the same way as SQRT was used above. Most Fortran systems will have about ten such *external functions*, larger systems as many as twenty-five.

A *function* is a subprogram which calculates a single value. The most used external functions follow.

EXP

The Fortran statement:

```
Y = EXP(X)
```

is equivalent to the algebraic expression:

$$y = e^x$$

where e is the base of natural logarithms, approximately 2.718. This *exponential function* is one much used in scientific and mathematical applications.

ALOG

This is a function used to compute natural logarithms of numbers. The statement:

X = ALOG(Y)

is the Fortran expression of:

$$x = \log_e y$$

Trigonometric functions—SIN, COS, ATAN

These are mathematical functions of angles, and when used in Fortran the angles must be expressed in radians. Degrees

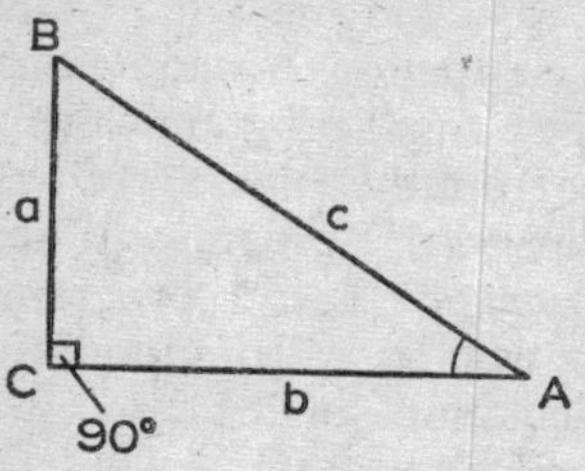

$$\sin A = \frac{a}{c}$$

$$\cos A = \frac{b}{c}$$

$$\tan A = \frac{a}{b} = \frac{\sin A}{\cos A}$$

$$\arctan\left(\frac{a}{b}\right) = A$$

Fig. 8.1

may be converted to radians by multiplying by 0.01745 (approximately). For those readers who have forgotten their trigonometry, Fig. 8.1 shows the functions.

'ATAN' is an abbreviation used for the term 'arctangent', or 'the angle whose tangent is . . .'. The tangent of an angle is the ratio of its sine to its cosine. ATAN enables us, given the angle's tangent, to compute its value in radians.

SQRT

The Fortran statement:

```
Y = SQRT (X)
```

is equivalent to the algebraic expression:

$$y = \sqrt{x}$$

and computes the value of the square root of the variable X as long as X is positive or zero. If X happens to be negative, the action which is taken depends on the Fortran compiler being used. In general, it is best to test the argument (X) before using the SQRT function to ensure that it is not negative; if it *does* turn out to be negative, you can then take whatever action seems appropriate before the SQRT function fails, possibly irrecoverably. A possible action might be the following:

```
      . . .
      IF (X) 10, 20, 20
   10 WRITE (3, 100) X
  100 FORMAT (19H0NEGATIVE ARGUMENT,
     *    20HFOR SQRT AT LABEL 10/
     *    15H VALUE OF X IS , E15.7)
      PAUSE 777
      . . .
   20 Y = SQRT (X)
      . . .
      etc.
```

Here, if the argument of SQRT is negative, this is detected by the arithmetic IF statement, and a message is printed. Notice the use of the E field specification, for the magnitude of the argument is not known. After the message has been printed, an identifiable PAUSE (777) occurs, and the user can give the operator specific instructions as to what is to be done if this happens.

Every Fortran function has at least one argument, placed inside the parentheses which follow the function name. In the case of the examples given so far, these arguments are real variables or expressions. Occasionally, they may be real constants, but this should be a rare occurrence. Variables may be subscripted. Examples of valid calls on library functions are the following:

```
A(9) = COS (B(17))
ASW4 = ALOG (D*BETA*ABLE(8))
V = SQRT (SIN (X-Z(8))
```

Note how, in the last example, the result of one function evaluation is used as the argument for another function.

Intrinsic library functions

Many computer installations will have more than the six external library functions described in the previous section. These are mathematical functions, but there exists another group—the intrinsic functions—which is used in exactly the same way but whose purpose is rather more one of 'house-keeping'—simple manipulation rather than calculation. Some of the more useful of these functions are described below.

ABS and IABS

These are used to obtain the absolute value of the argument: real for ABS and integer for IABS. By absolute value is meant the value which is obtained when the sign of the argument is ignored. For instance, ABS(3.43) and ABS(−3.43) will both deliver the value +3.43. Similarly, IABS(23) and IABS(−23) will both produce the value +23. Examples of use:

```
A = SQRT (ABS (X**2 − Y**2))
K = IABS (L*M + N)
```

AINT and INT

These are truncation functions: they produce the largest whole number less than or equal to the argument, the term 'less than' being interpreted as meaning 'in the direction of zero'. AINT produces a real result from a real argument, INT gives an integer result from a real argument. Thus, if X has the value −12.3, Y has the value 26.9, then:

```
A = AINT (X) assigns the value —12.0 to A
B = AINT (Y) assigns the value   26.0 to B
J =   INT (X) assigns the value —12   to J
K =   INT (Y) assigns the value   26   to K
```

AMOD and MOD

It often happens that the remainder resulting from a division is needed, and these functions will produce that value. AMOD expects real arguments and produces a real result, MOD expects integer arguments and gives an integer result.

The functions each require two arguments. AMOD (X, Y) computes the remainder when X is divided by Y. Thus, if X has the value 34.0 and Y is 7.0, Z = AMOD(X, Y) will assign the value 6.0 to Z. Similarly, if I has the value 15 and J is 6, the effect of N = MOD (I, J) is to assign the value 3 to the variable N. The sign of the remainder may be determined by applying the equivalent formula, which is for MOD or AMOD (a, b):

a — INT (a/b) * b

FLOAT and IFIX

Conversion between real and integer forms is provided by these functions. Each takes a single argument *the value of which is unchanged after the function has been evaluated.* The main use of these is to overcome the problems which may result from the fact that mixed-mode expressions are not allowed. For example,

```
AVRAGE = SUM / N
```

is not permitted, but

```
AVRAGE = SUM / FLOAT (N)
```

would be quite acceptable, since the value computed by FLOAT (N) is the real number corresponding to the integer value of N. So, if N had a value of 32, FLOAT (N) would produce the value 32.0.

In the same way, one could not normally write:

```
KOUNT = N * X + J
```

But the availability of conversion functions enables us to write:

```
KOUNT = N * IFIX (X) + J
```

which is perfectly valid. If X were of value 19.0, IFIX (X) would produce the value 19. In general, IFIX and INT may be used interchangeably.

There are a number of other useful intrinsic functions, but they are used less frequently than those mentioned and so will not be detailed here. They include functions for choosing the largest or smallest value from a list of variables, manipulating the signs of numbers, separating the real and imaginary parts of complex numbers, and so on. Full information will be found in the manual for the computer you are using, if you feel these functions may be useful to you.

Functions defined by the programmer

The user of Fortran has available to him a good selection of library functions, as the previous sections will have indicated, but it is not possible to provide for the complete needs of every user. Facilities are therefore provided to enable users to define functions to meet their own individual requirements. The simplest of these is the *statement function.*

Statement functions

Sometimes a program will call for a calculation to be performed a number of times, not in regular sequence, as might be the case if a DO loop were used, but now and again at random points in the program. Suppose, for example, that the following statements appear in a program at various unrelated places:

```
A = F*F + G*(F - G)
D(17) = B*B + S(1)*(B - S(1))
V = D(16)*D(16) + R(3)*(D(16) - R(3))
B = A*A + F*(A - F)
```

A careful examination of these four apparently quite different statements will reveal that they have essentially the same structure, in that the actual calculation is the same in every case: a value is squared and to the square is added the product of a second value and the difference between the two. Now we could, of course, write down each of these formulae each time it was needed at the appropriate point in the program. The result would be an efficient program, but quite a lot of effort is involved, especially if the formula is a long and involved one. An alternative is to reduce the effort required and, possibly, make rather more efficient use of the machine's storage capacity by writing out the calculation *once only*. We could then inform the system, every time this formula is needed, that it must use the one copy supplied, substituting the appropriate variables in the correct places.

This is permitted in Fortran. The definition is called a statement function, and it is used in the same way as the library functions dealt with previously. The word *statement* associated with these functions serves to emphasise the requirement that *the calculation specified must be capable of expression by means of a single Fortran statement.*

Suppose that we wish to use such a function. It will need to have a name, and this name will be constructed in accordance with the normal rules for naming variables. The first letter of the name is determined by the type of result produced by the function: for an integer result, one of the letters I, J, K, L, M or N; for a real result, one of the remaining letters of the alphabet. Assuming that our function is to produce a real result, let us call it CALC

The next step is to write the function definition which specifies the general form of the calculation to be performed. This is a suitable definition:

```
CALC (X, Y) = X*X + Y*(X − Y)
```

In this definition, X and Y are *dummy variables*. That is, they represent *an arithmetic expression* which may be substituted for them when the function is used during the execution of the program. The simplest arithmetic expression is, of course, a simple variable or constant.

Suppose now that we wish to write the first of the statements given as examples earlier. Instead of writing:

```
A = F*F + G*(F − G)
```

we need now only state:

```
A = CALC (F, G)
```

When this statement is encountered during the execution of the program, the effect will be as though the definition given above were substituted for CALC, with F substituted for X and G replacing Y throughout.

In a similar way, the other three statements become:

```
D(17) = CALC (B, S(1))
V = CALC (D(16), R(3))
B = CALC (A, F)
```

The variable names appearing inside the parentheses following the function name are those of the arguments of the function. The list of these arguments which appears in the *calling statement*—that is, the statement which calls for the evaluation of the function, as in the four examples given—must agree with that in the function definition in the order, type and number of variables. It would be quite wrong, for example, to write a call on CALC of the form:

```
W = CALC (J, F, U, D(12))
```

since the variables constituting the arguments here do not agree in number or type with those of the definition of CALC.

The definition of a statement function may be regarded as a template for a Fortran statement, rather than a normal executable statement. There are a number of points that need to be borne in mind when writing such definitions:

1. The definition of a statement function should immediately precede either the first executable statement of a program or another statement function definition.
2. Since the definition is not itself an instruction in the normal sense, it should not bear a statement number.
3. Subscripted variables may not be used on the right-hand side of a statement function definition.

4. The right-hand side of the definition may contain references to other functions. These may be library functions, programmer-defined external functions (see next section) or statement functions. If they are statement functions, they must have been defined before the attempt to call on them.

Function calls may be used in the same way as any other Fortran expression. We might have, for example:

```
IF (CALC (R, T)) 34, 10, 2
```

giving a branch to a destination determined by the evaluation of

```
R*R + T*(R - T)
```

They may be used as the arguments of other functions:

```
S(14) = SQRT (CALC (W, E(6)))
```

would be a perfectly valid statement. As usual, a little care must be taken to ensure that the parentheses are correctly balanced.

Function subprograms

These are external functions, like the library functions discussed earlier, the difference being that they are defined by the programmer to his own specification and are generally only available to him during the period of execution of his program.

A function subprogram is very similar in its use to the statement function, but there are one or two fundamental differences. In the first place, whereas the statement function forms a part of the program which uses it and is compiled at the same time, the function subprogram is a quite independent program and is compiled quite separately from the program which calls it. Secondly, the function subprogram may contain any number of Fortran statements, whereas a statement function is limited to being a single statement. Function subprograms are used when the amount of work required to be done cannot be specified by a single Fortran statement.

Function subprograms are named in the same way as statement functions or simple variables. If their result is to be real, the name starts with any letter *other than* I, J, K, L, M or N. If the result is to be an integer (in the strict Fortran sense), the name should begin with one of I, J, K, L, M or N. It is best to avoid names such as SIN or COS, because of the possibility of confusion with library functions. The compiler should not get confused, but other users looking through your programs almost certainly will!

Remember that function subprograms are programs in their own right which are physically separate from the calling program but may be referenced by this program when required. The way in which this is achieved will be explained shortly. Let us consider an example.

It is required to produce a function subprogram which has three arguments, A, B and C. If A^2 exceeds the product of B and C, the value of the function is to be 1.0; if the product exceeds the square, a value of 5.0 should be returned; and if the product is equal to the square, the result should be 0.0.

If the name of the function is to be TEST, the following would be a suitable function subprogram to perform the actions specified:

```
   FUNCTION TEST (A, B, C)
   IF (A*A – B*C) 1, 2, 3
 1 TEST = 5.0
   GO TO 4
 2 TEST = 0.0
   GO TO 4
 3 TEST = 1.0
 4 RETURN
   END
```

There are two new statement types here: that which begins 'FUNCTION', and the 'RETURN' statement. Let us consider these in more detail before analysing the program.

FUNCTION TEST (A, B, C): the word 'FUNCTION' tells the compiler that this program is a function subprogram. It will be referred to by the name TEST, and since this is the name of a real variable we infer that the function delivers a real result. Following the name comes a list of dummy arguments, enclosed in parentheses. When the function is called, these will be replaced, wherever they occur in the subprogram, by the actual arguments which will be given in the calling statement.

When a subprogram is called into action from a main program (or, possibly, from another subprogram), a link is established between the two programs which, you will recall, were separately compiled. Among other information, this link specifies the exact point in the calling program from which the reference to the subprogram was made. The effect of the RETURN statement is to extract this *return address* from wherever it has been stored, and to branch back into the calling program at the instruction immediately following that which called the subprogram into action. Obviously, then, the RETURN statement should be the last one executed in the evaluation of a function. Note that this is not the same as saying that it should be the last statement of the function subprogram, though, as it happens, this is the case in our example (excepting the END statement, which is not executable but an indicator to the compiler of the extent of the subprogram).

The remainder of the subprogram is self-explanatory, though the use of the variable TEST is a little unusual perhaps. The name of the function is used just as though it were an ordinary variable (this is why we have to be careful in our choice of function name), and the final result of the function evaluation must be assigned to this variable. This is the way the result is linked back to the calling program.

A point of style is worth mentioning: although there may be as many RETURN statements as is felt necessary, only one is given here, and the three points from which an exit might have been made converge onto this single statement by, in two cases, GO TO statements. In general, this tends to make a program more easily understood by the reader than having multiple exit points, and it is usually accepted as being good programming practice.

Reference to this function is made in exactly the same way as if it were a statement function or a library function. A typical call on the function might be:

```
S = R + TEST (X, Y(I), ZETA)
```

The following is a description of the effect of this statement. The statements of the calling program would be executed until this line was reached, and we assume that values would have been assigned to R, X, ZETA and the appropriate element of the array Y. Recognising a call on the function TEST, control is then passed to the first executable statement of the subprogram. This is executed as though the dummy variables had been replaced by the corresponding actual variables which appear in the call shown above:

```
  IF (X*X – Y(I)*ZETA) 1, 2, 3
1 TEST = 5.0
  GO TO 4
2 TEST = 0.0
  GO TO 4
3 TEST = 1.0
4 CONTINUE
```

would be an equivalent statement sequence. So the variable TEST acquires a value of 1.0, 0.0 or 5.0, depending on the relative values of X, Y(I) and ZETA.

Let us assume that the value assigned to the function name

is 5.0. Control is returned to the calling program, and the statement becomes, in effect,

```
S = R + 5.0
```

which is executed in the normal manner, control then passing to the next statement in sequence.

It is again required by the system that the actual arguments of the function shall agree in order, number and type with the dummy arguments.

Subscripted variables may be used inside the function subprogram, and care should be taken to ensure that any which do appear also have a DIMENSION declaration. The dummy arguments may be the *names* of arrays, if this is found to be necessary, but they should not be subscripted in the list following the function name. The following example of a function subprogram which forms the sum of the elements of the array A should help to clarify some of the points made.

```
   FUNCTION ADEMUP (A, N)
   DIMENSION A(1)
   ADEMUP = 0.0
   DO 10 I=1, N
      ADEMUP = ADEMUP + A(I)
10 CONTINUE
   RETURN
   END
```

A typical call of this function might be in the following context

```
...
DIMENSION X(100)
...
XMEAN = ADEMUP (X, 100)/100.0
...
```

One point in this example which may be found rather confusing is the dimensioning of the array A in the subprogram:

```
DIMENSION A(1)
```

It is important to realise that A is a dummy variable, and at the time the subprogram is written the programmer may well have no idea how large the array may be. The function can be used to sum any number of elements of the array, by adjusting the value of the argument N on entry. But the fact is that the array already exists when the subprogram is called. Storage for the array will have been reserved by an appropriate DIMENSION statement in the calling program. It follows that our subprogram's DIMENSION statement must have another purpose. It does not reserve storage. The only reason for having it is to inform the compiler that A is, in fact, an array. If this were not done, there would be the chance of interpreting 'A(I)' as a call of the function A with an actual argument I. This will happen if we omit the DIMENSION statement. The dimensions given are unimportant, as long as they do not exceed those of the array which constitutes the actual argument, and so 1 would seem to be as good a choice as any other value.

The function may make use of *local* variables, which will be 'known' only within the subprogram—I, in the above function subprogram, is an example of a local variable. Local arrays may sometimes be needed. When this is the case, the correct dimensions must, of course, be given in the DIMENSION statement, for it will be necessary to reserve the right number of memory cells since the array has not been mentioned elsewhere.

The arguments of a function may be expressions, as well as simple variables. To give an example, the following would be a valid call on the function INTER:

```
MOST = N(1) – INTER (M, J/3, 4*N(2))
```

and the function subprogram could start in this way:

```
FUNCTION INTER (I, K, L)
```

Note that each of the expressions used as arguments for the function agrees in type with the dummy arguments of the definition. Here is another example of a different function:

```
FUNCTION SPAN (X, N, Y)
. . . etc.
```

A valid call on this function would be the following:

```
P = SPAN (A, 2*I/3, P+Q)
```

See the agreement in type, as well as order, between the actual and the dummy arguments. The first and last arguments are real, the second is of integer type.

Three final rules for the function subprogram:

1. The name of the function *must*, at some point in the function subprogram, appear as the left-hand side of an assignment statement: in other words, the function is intended to deliver a single value to the calling program, and this value must be assigned to the function at some point in the function subprogram.
2. A function subprogram must have *at least one* dummy argument. A statement such as the following:

   ```
   FUNCTION CHECK
   ```

   would be invalid, for no arguments are shown. Even on the rare occasion when no arguments are needed, it will be necessary to have a *dummy* dummy argument!
3. It is not permitted to equivalence together two or more dummy arguments.

Subroutine subprograms

We come now to the last of the different types of subprogram which will be considered in this book. This is the *subroutine*, and it differs only in slight detail from the function subprogram dealt with in the last section. The primary difference is that, whereas the function returns a single value to the calling program, the subroutine is able to return any number of values.

The mechanism by which values are returned is a little different, in the case of the subroutine, from that of the function subprogram. You will remember that the name of the function is used as a variable to forge the link between the calling program and the function. We say that functions are called *implicitly*, just by quoting their names and an appropriate list of arguments in an arithmetic statement.

The subroutine is organised a little differently. In the first place, it must be called *explicitly*—a special Fortran statement is used to initiate the actions of a subroutine. Secondly, the results computed by a subroutine are transmitted back to the calling program by means of the argument list, no value being assigned to the name of the subroutine. The first statement of the subroutine differs slightly from that of the function, but the idea of the routine's being an independent program, compiled separately from the calling program, remains the same for subroutines as for functions.

Consider the following example of an application of a subroutine. At a number of points in a program, it is required that the value and position of the smallest element of an array should be determined. Several different arrays, of different sizes, are involved, so that the argument list will need to contain basic dimension information. The following is a subroutine subprogram which will give the desired result:

```
      SUBROUTINE SMALL (A, N, X, I)
C * A IS THE ARRAY NAME
C * N IS THE NUMBER OF ELEMENTS IN A
C * X WILL, ON EXIT, CONTAIN THE VALUE
C *   OF THE SMALLEST ELEMENT OF A
```

```
C * I WILL, ON EXIT, INDICATE THE POSITION
C *    OF THE SMALLEST ELEMENT
       DIMENSION A(1)
C * X AND I ARE FIRST GIVEN THEIR
C *    STARTING VALUES
       X = A(1)
       I = 1
C * NOW WE COMPARE EACH ELEMENT OF
C *    A WITH X IN TURN. WHEN A VALUE
C *    WHICH IS LESS THAN X TURNS UP,
C *    THE VALUE OF X IS CHANGED AND
C *    THE VALUE OF I ADJUSTED
       DO 10 J = 2, N
          IF (X .LT. A(J)) GO TO 10
          X = A(J)
          I = J
   10  CONTINUE
       RETURN
       END
```

Notice how the results are returned to the calling program: there are two arguments, X and I, which are given values during the execution of the subroutine. Similarly, the two arguments A and N give the subroutine the information it needs to perform its task. J is a local variable. A and N are sometimes termed *inputs*, X and I *outputs* of the subroutine. Sometimes an input argument will have its value changed by the subroutine, in which case it may be termed an *input-output* argument.

The name of our example subroutine is SMALL. This is contained in the first statement of the subprogram, the form of which should be carefully noted. A SUBROUTINE statement must always be first in a subroutine subprogram. As in the case of the function, control is returned to the calling program by means of the RETURN statement.

The subroutine is called from the main program by means

of a special type of statement, which, in the case of the example given, might be as follows:

```
CALL SMALL (VALL, 100, RESULT, IPOS)
```

Again it will be seen that the actual arguments agree in number, order and type with the dummy arguments of the subprogram. When the CALL statement is executed, control is passed to the first statement of the subroutine. Wherever A is mentioned in the subroutine, VALL will be substituted; for X, RESULT will be understood; N and I will be replaced by 100 and IPOS respectively. The subroutine will then be executed as if it were any other Fortran program, and when the RETURN statement is reached control will be returned to the main program at the statement following the CALL statement. The values of RESULT and IPOS will be the values last assigned to X and I in the subroutine.

Note the need for an END statement to indicate to the compiler the physical end of the subprogram. As with functions, the actual arguments may be any expression. Occasionally, a subroutine will not need any arguments. When this happens, it is quite permissible to omit the argument list, and its surrounding parentheses. Here is a trivial example:

```
      SUBROUTINE PAGE
C * THIS ROUTINE POSITIONS THE CARRIAGE
C * OF THE LINE PRINTER AT THE HEAD OF
C * A NEW PAGE
      WRITE (3, 100)
  100 FORMAT ( 1H1)
      RETURN
      END
```

A suitable call for this subroutine would be:

```
      CALL PAGE
```

It is not necessary that a subroutine without arguments should be trivial. Later we shall see an example of one which performs much more complex calculation.

Overall job structure

A Fortran *job* consists of exactly one main program and as many subprograms, functions or subroutines as are considered necessary by the programmer. Usually, the main program will be positioned at the head of the job, so that it is compiled first. No difficulty should be experienced in deciding how functions are to be used. The defining statement for a statement function is, as has already been indicated, placed right at the head of the program (or subprogram) which refers to it, before any executable statements. Note that, if the same statement function is referenced in two different program units (main program or subprogram), it will need to be defined in both of them. If this occurs across several program units, you may consider it better to rewrite it as a function subprogram. The following represents a typical Fortran job, but the precise make-up of such a program deck will often depend on the compiler or computer system being used, so look at the reference manual for details.

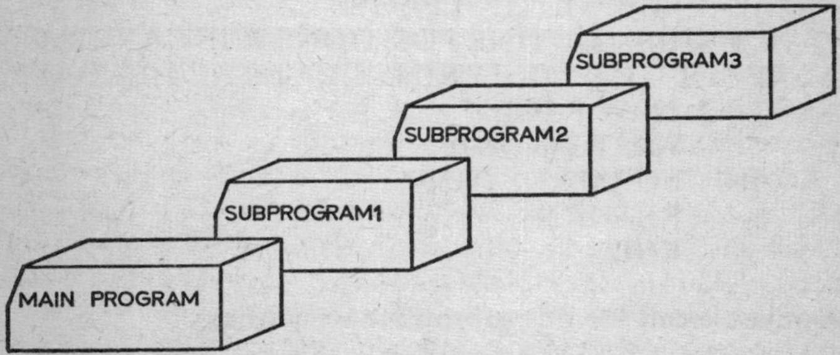

Fig. 8.2

The COMMON statement

In the examples given previously involving subprograms, the transfer of data between the calling program and the subprogram has been explicit, in that there has been an argument list. The idea of *common storage*—that is, an area of memory common to both calling and called program unit—was introduced so that this transfer of information could be effected in an implicit manner. Its use means that argument lists can, in certain circumstances, be dispensed with, and the overall result is usually a more efficient program in terms of both storage usage and running time.

When a program and its associated subprograms are executed, it is usual for both the main program and its subprograms to be held in the machine's memory at the same time. This may not be possible in the case of very large Fortran jobs, but we shall consider the more usual situation. The main program will occupy one part of the store, and the subroutines will each occupy a separate section of the store. Each program unit will have an area of memory allocated to its use for holding the variables and constants which it needs to refer to. This situation is illustrated in Fig. 8.3(*a*).

An alternative would be such that, while the main program and subprograms still occupy different parts of memory, the variables—or some of them, at least—are assigned to storage locations in such a way that those of the calling program occupy the same places as those in the called subprograms. This is shown in Fig. 8.3(*b*). This is an instance of the use of common storage.

Obviously, if two variables occupy a location in common storage, their values at any given instant will be identical. Thus, any changes in value which occur in the subprogram will be automatically propagated into the calling program, and *vice-versa*.

Variables are placed into common storage by using the COMMON statement. The example which follows shows the statements needed to ensure that two arrays called TERMS and BEZT, each having thirty elements, defined in different program units, share the same memory space.

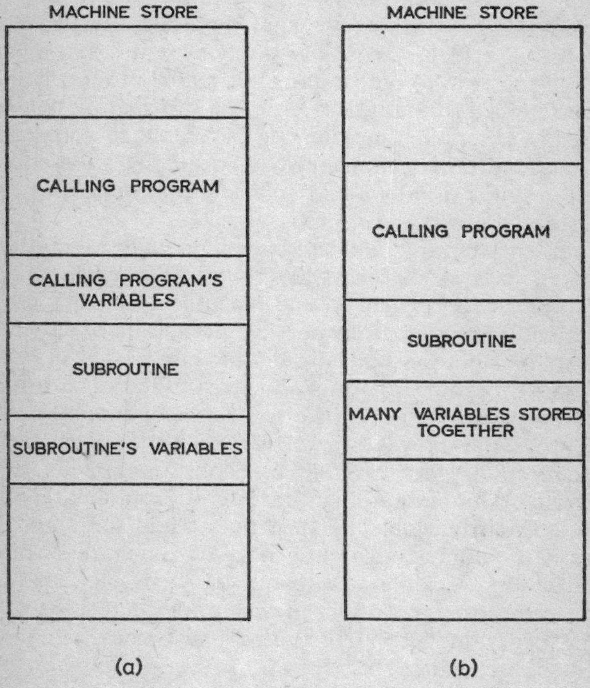

Fig. 8.3

In the calling program:

```
DIMENSION TERMS (30)
COMMON TERMS
```

It is possible to economise on writing and punching effort somewhat by making the COMMON statement do the work of a DIMENSION statement also. The following statement will have the same effect as the two given above:

```
COMMON TERMS (30)
```

In the called program:

```
DIMENSION BEZT (30)
COMMON BEZT
```

or, perhaps, simply:

```
COMMON BEZT (30)
```

The effect is to assign TERMS and BEZT to a common storage area. Any alteration in value of an element of TERMS causes the exactly similar change to the corresponding element of BEZT. There is thus no need for the name of either array to appear in an argument list.

Simple variables may be allocated space in common storage in just the same way, and any number of variable names may appear in a COMMON statement. The important point is that common storage is allocated on a first-come, first-served basis: the variables at corresponding points of two COMMON statements in different program units will be allocated the same location. For instance, in the calling program:

```
COMMON X, Y, Z(30), P(12), Q
```

has the effect of reserving the next forty-five real storage locations in the common area for X, Y, Z, P and Q.

In the called program, we might have:

```
COMMON A, B, C(30), D(12), E
```

which will assign A, B, C, D and E to the same storage area.

Yet another program unit might be interested only in the fifth variable in the common area—that called previously Q or E. The following COMMON statement would fit such a need:

```
COMMON SPACE(44), R
```

The dummy array SPACE has been introduced to space over the forty-four real storage locations which precede that which will be referred to as R and which is elsewhere known as Q or E.

There is an apparent similarity between the COMMON statement and the EQUIVALENCE statement dealt with in Chapter 7. However, COMMON is used to bring about the sharing of memory resources *between* program units, whereas EQUIVALENCE causes memory to be shared *within* a program unit. The two can interact to some extent in that a variable in common storage may be equivalenced to one which is not. In such a case, the second is automatically brought into common storage. Any such equivalence operation which increases the common area in the forward direction is acceptable, but if the effect is to attempt to move backwards the start of the area of common storage the operation is an illegal one. The following two examples may serve to clarify this point.

```
COMMON X(10)
DIMENSION Y(10)
EQUIVALENCE (X(3), Y(1))
```

The effect of this statement sequence is to bring the whole of the array Y into the common area, though a consideration of the COMMON statement alone would not indicate that any such thing was intended. Fig. 8.4(*a*) illustrates the situation. Extension of the common area is away from its origin, and the action is acceptable.

```
COMMON X(10)
DIMENSION Y(10)
EQUIVALENCE (X(3), Y(4))
```

Despite its very similar appearance to the previous example, this sequence is quite unacceptable. If it were possible to achieve this equivalence, the bringing of the array Y into the common area would involve its extension backwards beyond X(1). Such backward extension is forbidden. See Fig. 8.4(*b*).

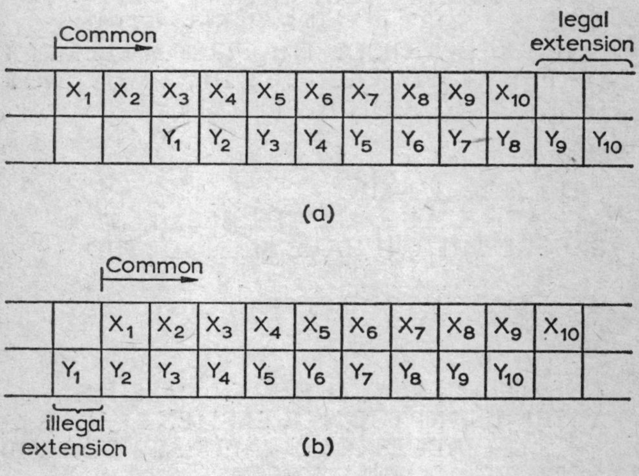

Fig. 8.4

To finish this chapter, let us consider one final example of a subroutine, but in this case the transfer of arguments will be achieved by the use of common storage. It is designed to sort the elements of the array VALUES, which has N elements, into ascending numerical order, using a very simple algorithm which is summarised in the flowchart of Fig. 8.5. The technique is one of linear selection and exchanging: on the first scan through the array, the smallest element is found and brought to the top (i.e. first) position. Scanning then starts again at the second position, and the process is repeated. Each scan involves the examination of one element less than the previous scan, until only two are left. When these have been dealt with, the process is complete.

```
      SUBROUTINE SORT
      COMMON N, VALUES(1000)
C * THIS IS A SORT BY LINEAR SELECTION
C * AND EXCHANGE OF THE FIRST N ELEMENTS
C * OF THE ARRAY VALUES, WHICH MUST NOT
C * CONTAIN MORE THAN 1000 ELEMENTS
      NM1 = N - 1
C * POSITION OF LAST-BUT-ONE ELEMENT
      DO 20 I = 1, NM1
C * AT EACH STAGE, ALL THE ELEMENTS
C * BEFORE THE ITH HAVE BEEN SORTED
        IP1 = I + 1
C * IP1 INDICATES THE START POINT
C * FOR THE NEXT SCAN
        DO 10 J = IP1, N
C * AND, OF COURSE, THE SCAN FINISHES
C * AFTER USING THE NTH ELEMENT
          IF (VALUES(I) .LE. VALUES(J)) GO TO 10
C * NOTE WE DO NOT EXCHANGE IF THE
C * ELEMENTS ARE OF EQUAL VALUE
          X = VALUES(I)
          VALUES(I) = VALUES(J)
          VALUES(J) = X
 10     CONTINUE
 20   CONTINUE
      RETURN
C * ALL VALUES SORTED INTO
C * ASCENDING NUMERICAL ORDER
      END
```

The subroutine is called SORT, and has no explicit arguments.

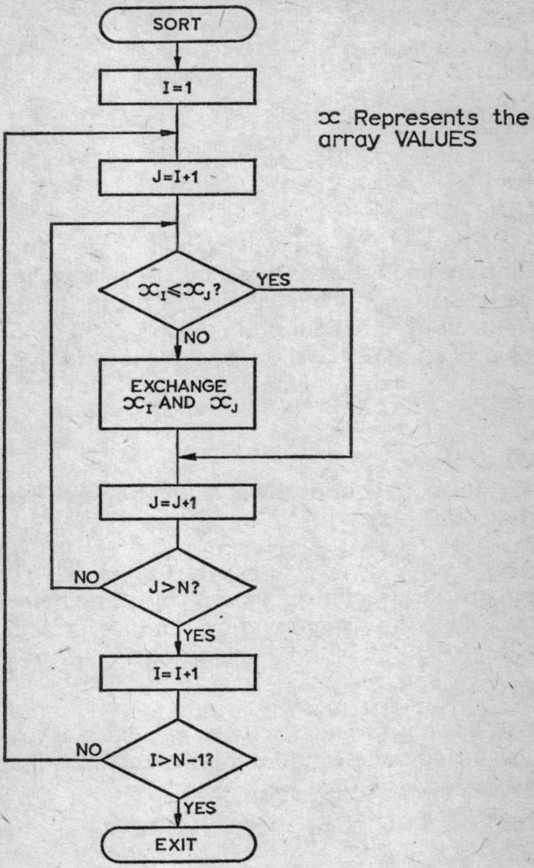
SORT
I=1
J=I+1
x_I ≤ x_J ?
YES
NO
EXCHANGE
x_I AND x_J
J=J+1
NO
J>N?
YES
I=I+1
NO
I>N−1?
YES
EXIT
x Represents the
array VALUES

Fig. 8.5

Any calling program would need to have corresponding COMMON statements:

e.g. COMMON NEL, DATA(1000)

and a calling statement:

```
CALL SORT
```

Since DATA and VALUES, NEL and N are held in corresponding common storage locations, any change in one is a change in the other. Thus, filling DATA in the main program sets up VALUES for the subprogram, and the reordering of VALUES in the subprogram is, in fact, sorting DATA for the main program.

Exercises

1. Write down, in your own words, the rules for the naming of functions.

2. What are the essential differences between statement functions, function subprograms and subroutine subprograms?

3. The following formula is to be evaluated a number of times during the execution of a program, using different variables on each occasion:

$$t^2 + u^3 + v^4$$

   Write a suitable Fortran function, and give a reason for your choice.

4. The cotangent of an angle is defined as the ratio of the cosine to the sine of the angle:

$$\cot x = \frac{\cos x}{\sin x}$$

Write a statement to calculate the cotangent of an angle (called ANGLE) expressed in degrees. The value of the cotangent is to be assigned to a variable called COT.

5. A one-dimensional array is called WEEK and has seven elements. Write a subroutine subprogram, with no argument list, to add together all the values in WEEK and divide the result by 7.0, finally assigning the result to WEEK(1). Write also the necessary Fortran statement(s) which will be needed in the main program to invoke the subroutine.

6. A function is required to compare the values of two variables, X and Y. If X is equal to Y, a value of 3.0 is to be returned to the calling program; if X is not equal to Y but *is* equal to a third variable, Z, the value to be returned is 4.0; 6.0 is the value to be returned otherwise. Write a suitable function to perform these operations.

7. True or false?

   (*a*) Functions must always have arguments.
   (*b*) Subroutines must always have arguments.
   (*c*) Arguments may be transferred to a subroutine either implicitly (using COMMON) or explicitly (using an argument list), but not both.
   (*d*) A function name may have up to six characters.
   (*e*) A subroutine name may appear in an expression, just like the name of any other variable.
   (*f*) The subroutine's name is used to transfer the result back to the calling program.

8. Locate the errors in the following Fortran statements:

(*a*) FUNCTION ABSOL (A B N)
(*b*) DEAF (T, Y, P) = C*C + D*D + C*D
(*c*) IF (WRDTF) (U, V, W) 12, 34, 35
(*d*) SUBROUTINE CALCULATION
(*e*) FUNCTION READF (D(9), B, M)

9 Further aspects of Fortran

In the chapters leading up to this one, the basic ideas of the Fortran language have been studied. It has been necessary to omit a lot of the fine detail, but you should by now have a broad idea of the structure of the language as a whole, be able to write simple programs and be able to adapt your knowledge to any specific Fortran system with which you may come into contact. A book such as this can hope to do no more than give an idea of the possibilities, leaving the reader to follow those paths which have most appeal.

However, there are one or two features of Fortran which, although not essential, are often used and should be known to any prospective programmer. They should be available on any computer claiming to have an implementation of ANSI Fortran (the American standard) but, inevitably, some systems will not be able to supply them all—a remark which also applies to those features mentioned earlier.

Logical variables

Any logical expression can have only one of two possible values. It may be *true* or, if it is not, it must be *false*. These are values, just as numeric and Hollerith constants are values, and they can be stored in memory in the same way. However, it is necessary that they be held in memory cells reserved for the specific purpose of storing logical values.

The two logical constants are designated:

.TRUE. and .FALSE.

Note that, as in the case of the relational operators and logical operators discussed in Chapter 5, these values are delimited by points.

A variable is defined as being of the logical type, and thus distinguished from integers and real numbers, by its appearance in a *type declaration* statement at the beginning of the program unit in which it is used. For example, to declare the variable F6A (which would otherwise be assumed to be a real variable) as of logical type, the following type declaration is needed:

```
LOGICAL F6A
```

After this has been done, it is possible to assign logical values to the variable, either directly, as in the following example:

```
F6A = .FALSE.
```

or by the evaluation of a logical expression:

```
F6A = S .LE. G
```

In the first case, F6A is assigned the value of the logical constant, and thus acquires the value *false*. In the second case, the value assigned depends on the algebraic relationship between the variables S and G. If S is less than or equal in value to G, F6A will be assigned the value *true*, since that is the value of the expression. If not, the value *false* will be assigned.

Logical variables may be used in the logical IF statement. A common application is that in which a particular action needs to be taken only on the first time around a loop. In such a case, a sequence such as the following may occur in a program:

```
LOGICAL FIRST
. . .
FIRST = .TRUE.
. . .
DO 10 I = 1, N
IF (.NOT. FIRST) GO TO 5
. . .
```

```
        action to be performed
        on the first loop only
        ...
        FIRST = .FALSE.
        GO TO 10
      5 ...
        normal loop action
        ...
     10 CONTINUE
        etc.
```

The use of '.NOT.' here helps to preserve a natural flow in the program structure which would be lost if a direct test of the type:

```
    IF (FIRST) GO TO ...
```

were used, involving a separated block of code to deal with the special case.

Other type declarations

Throughout the book, so far, we have stuck to the convention that integer variable names begin with one of the letters I, J, K, L, M or N, and that real variable names begin with one of the remaining letters of the alphabet. The same convention has applied to the choosing of names for functions. These are 'default' options, which are applied so long as nothing is specified, in the program, to the contrary. There is, however, provision to override the convention if the need arises, and this is done by means of a type statement similar to that used to declare logical variables. Suppose, for instance, that we have a variable whose name is NCA, but that we wish this variable to be treated as a real quantity in the program. All that is needed is a type statement of the form:

```
    REAL NCA
```

which informs the compiler that the variable NCA, although apparently of integer type, is to be treated as of real type for the whole of the program unit in which the declaration appears.

In exactly the same way, apparently real variables can be declared to be integers. Suppose that the variables A, B and COUNT are reasonable names to have chosen, but that they are required to represent integers. The statement we need is this:

```
INTEGER A, B, COUNT
```

and this will achieve the required change. Notice that as many variable names as are needed may appear in one type declaration, and that they should be separated by commas.

If it happens that the results being obtained are not sufficiently precise, it is possible to increase the number of significant figures in a real number. Each variable to which this applies must be separately mentioned in a DOUBLE PRECISION declaration. This feature can be very useful when work has to be carried out to a high degree of accuracy. Many engineering calculations need this sort of facility, but it is unlikely to be of much value to the beginner in programming. A typical declaration would be:

```
DOUBLE PRECISION X, Y, Z
```

Finally, variables may be declared as COMPLEX:

```
COMPLEX P, Q, R
```

A complex number has two parts, known as the real and the imaginary parts of the number. Thus each number declared complex will take up as much space as two ordinary real numbers. Electrical engineers probably form the largest single group of people to whom complex numbers have any great significance. A detailed treatment will be found in appropriate textbooks.

There are means of representing both double precision and

complex constants in Fortran programs, but they will not be dealt with here. They have little significance unless a computer is to be used, in which case their form may be checked with the system Fortran manual.

Subprograms revisited

It has been pointed out several times that the type of the value returned by a function subprogram can be determined by checking the first letter of the function name, since it conforms to the naming convention for variables. Having introduced REAL, INTEGER, LOGICAL, DOUBLE PRECISION and COMPLEX, it can now be stated that these words can be prefixed to the word FUNCTION to ensure that the result of the computation is of the type specified.

For example, suppose that we have a function subprogram called CALC which, since its name starts with C, would normally be expected to return a real value to the calling program. The first instruction of the subprogram would, in that case, be:

```
FUNCTION CALC(A, B, N)
```

where A, B and N are the arguments of the function.

To make this function return an integer value to the calling program, it would need to be modified somewhat:

```
INTEGER FUNCTION CALC (A, B, N)
```

The same principle is used to change the apparent type of any function subprogram. Thus, a normally integer function called MEAN can be made to return a real value by the statement at the head of the function:

```
REAL FUNCTION MEAN (X, N)
```

where, again, X and N are the dummy arguments of the subprogram.

Exactly the same applies when a LOGICAL, COMPLEX or DOUBLE PRECISION result is needed. For example:

```
      LOGICAL FUNCTION LEAPYR (YEAR)
      INTEGER YEAR
C * THIS IS A FUNCTION WHICH RETURNS
C * THE VALUE .TRUE. IF 'YEAR' IS
C * A LEAP YEAR, .FALSE. OTHERWISE
      LEAPYR = .FALSE.
      IF (MOD (YEAR, 4) .NE. 0) GO TO 10
      LEAPYR = .TRUE.
      IF (MOD (YEAR, 100).N.E. 0) GO TO 10
      IF (MOD (YEAR, 400).E.Q. 0) GO TO 10
      LEAPYR = .FALSE.
   10 RETURN
      END
```

It is important to note that, when this facility is used, the name of the function must *also* appear in the appropriate type declaration in the calling program.

When a statement function is used, the type of the function can be declared in exactly the same way as that of any other variable. One example should serve to illustrate this:

```
INTEGER COUNT              type declaration
. . .
COUNT (I) = I + 1          function definition
. . .
K = L + COUNT (K)          function call
. . .
```

It is quite possible for the name of a subprogram to appear as an actual argument of the call of another subprogram. When this happens, the calling program needs to be informed of the fact, so that there will be no confusion between the name of the argument and that of an ordinary variable. So the argument is declared to be the name of a function in an EXTERNAL statement, placed at the head of the *calling* program. The example which follows should make the idea clear. TRIG is a function subprogram which can act to return a value derived from either the sine or the cosine of its argument, A. Which it is depends on the actual argument in the calling program which replaces the dummy argument F when the program is run.

```
      FUNCTION TRIG (A, F)
      R = A/57.1745
C * CONVERTS A TO RADIANS
      TRIG = 1.0 – F (R) * F (R)
      RETURN
      END
```

In the main program, TRIG might be used in the following way:

```
VALUE = 1.0/(1.0 – TRIG (THETA, SIN))
```

The effect of the call on TRIG will be to associate THETA with A and F with SIN, so that, after conversion of THETA to radians, the computed value is $1 - \sin^2\theta$, which is returned to the calling program.

An alternative main program sequence might have been:

```
P = TRIG(ALPHA, COS)
```

which would cause the value of $1 - \cos^2\alpha$ to be assigned to P.

The problem, looking at things from the compiler's point of view, is that it has no means of deciding whether SIN and COS as used in the actual arguments are simple real variables or the names of library functions (as is intended). Since the main program and the subprogram are compiled without reference to one another, there is no way in which the compiler can determine the real context of these names.

It follows that the programmer must specify this, and he does so by including the statement:

```
EXTERNAL SIN, COS
```

at the head of the main program, which informs the compiler that the variables SIN and COS are, in fact, the names of functions *external to* this particular program unit. The EXTERNAL statement should precede all executable statements and statement function definitions.

Initial values

It is often useful to have values assigned to some of a program's variables at the beginning of execution of a program unit. This can save execution time where, otherwise, a long string of simple assignments might be needed. For instance, if it is required to assign the values 1.3, 2.7, 10, 16 to the variables A, B, I and J respectively, the simple possibility is the following:

```
A = 1.3
B = 2.7
I = 10
J = 16
. . .
```

But this will require time for execution at run time and, furthermore, can be very tedious to write and punch when the list is a long one. The alternative is to use a *data initialisation* statement, of which the following is an example:

```
DATA A, B, I, J / 1.3, 2.7, 10, 16 /
```

The effect of such a statement is to ensure that, at the time the program is brought into memory for execution, the values given are assigned to their respective variables.

The general form of the statement, which should precede

all executable statements and statement function definitions, is:

DATA *lvars* / *lvals* /, *lvars* / *lvals* /, . . . etc.

where *lvars* represents a list of variable names, *lvals* represents a list of values, and the values are assigned to the variables in the strict order of their appearance. The variables may be subscripted. The last list of values must be terminated by a slash (/), but no terminal comma is needed. As many pairs of lists as are required may appear in the statement, and a single variable name or value is sufficient to constitute a list. The example DATA statement given above could be rephrased in a number of ways. Here are two of them:

```
DATA A / 1.3 /, B / 2.7 /, I / 10 /, J / 16 /
DATA A, B / 1.3, 2.7 /, I, J / 10, 16 /
```

The most compact method is probably that in which there is a single list of variables and the corresponding list of values.

Exercises

1. It is desired to use all the following variable names as integer variables, without changing them in any way. Write a single Fortran statement which will allow this to be done:

   KAN, LOO, ANT, Y, XRETY, MONO, STEREO, QUADRO, D7, E2R, PIN

2. If a variable X is greater than another variable Y, a logical variable called Z is to be assigned the value .TRUE., otherwise Z should receive the value .FALSE. Write suitable statements for this, including any necessary type declarations.

3. What, if anything, is wrong with each of the following statements, or sequences of statements?

   (*a*) LOGICAL A
   A = 3.0
   (*b*) REAL N
   M = A * N + J
   (*c*) REAL FUNCTION ARTHUR (AA, AB, AC)
   (*d*) IF (C .LE. D) 3, 6, 8
   (*e*) INTEGER V, OA, D
   OA = .TRUE.

10 Some other languages

Earlier in this book, it was stated that Fortran was only one of a number of programming languages which have been developed over the relatively short period since the appearance of the digital computer. For a number of reasons, Fortran and one or two others have become more popular than the remainder. Among the more important alternatives to Fortran are Algol 60 and PL/1, and COBOL is probably the most important language in the business world.

COBOL has a rather specialised format, though it is not a difficult language to learn, especially after a little experience of programming in another high-level language. However, we shall consider in this section only Algol 60 (which will be abbreviated to Algol), Fortran and PL/1, and will develop a program in each language. These three programs will each be a solution to the same simple problem, so that comparisons between the languages can be drawn. No attempt is made to teach Algol or PL/1—it is intended to give the flavour of each language only, and to show some similarities and differences.

Let us emphasise that the *principles* of programming remain the same, regardless of the language being used. This is analogous to saying that, if two people are having a conversation, the content of what they say to one another does not depend to any extent on the language which is used, so long as they both understand it, of course. All that has been said about flowcharting and the basic principles of programming is fundamental.

The problem

Let us choose a simple problem for our comparative programming exercise. We have an array of values, which we may call X, with appropriate subscripts. Associated with each X value is a *weight*, W, by which it is to be multiplied. The objective is to form the sum of all the weighted values, and to divide this by the sum of the X values, the result being called A.

$$A = \frac{W_1X_1 + W_2X_2 + W_3X_3 + \ldots + W_nX_n}{X_1 + \quad X_2 + \quad X_3 + \ldots + \quad X_n}$$

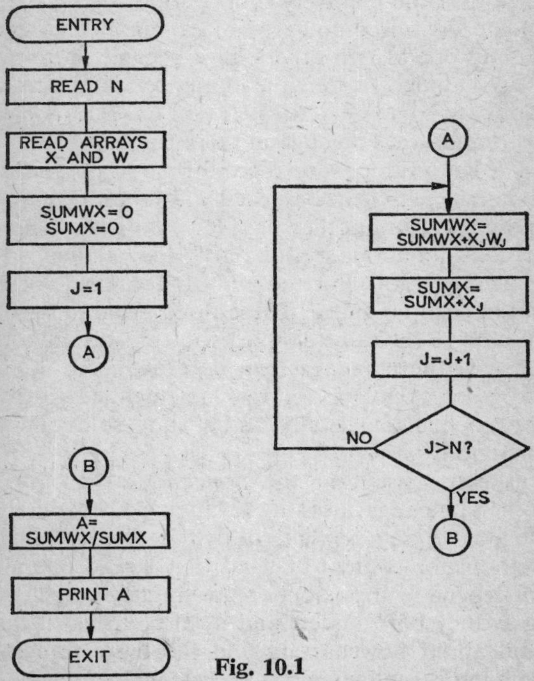

Fig. 10.1

We shall assume that the number of values to be considered will vary from run to run, but will never exceed 30.

Fig. 10.1 is a flowchart for the solution of this problem. As you can see, it is quite straightforward.

Fortran solution

With our newly acquired knowledge of the language, it should not be difficult to write a suitable Fortran program. Why don't you try before checking your answer against that given below?

```
      DIMENSION X(30), W(30)
C * INPUT NUMBER OF VALUES
      READ (2, 1) N
    1 FORMAT (I2)
C * NOW INPUT THE VALUES AND WEIGHTS
      READ (2, 2) (X(I), W(I), I = 1, N)
    2 FORMAT (2F10.0)
C * CLEAR THE SUMS INITIALLY
      SUMWX = 0.0
      SUMX = 0.0
      DO 3 J = 1, N
C * ADD TO SUM OF WEIGHTED VALUES
          SUMWX = SUMWX + X(J) * W(J)
C * ADD TO SUM OF X VALUES
          SUMX = SUMX + X(J)
    3 CONTINUE
C * COMPUTE QUOTIENT REQUIRED
      A = SUMWX / SUMX
      WRITE (3, 4) A
    4 FORMAT (10X, 10HRESULTbISb, F9.3)
      CALL EXIT
      END
```

This program could be written in a rather more efficient manner, but it has been given in its present form deliberately to improve its clarity. It should be almost self-explanatory, especially when read in conjunction with Fig. 10.1. Let us now consider another solution, this time using Algol 60 as our programming language.

Algol solution

There are a number of differences between Fortran and Algol, but a great number of similarities also.

```
begin integer n;
   comment until we have the value of n, we do not know
           how much storage the arrays will need, so we
           first read it;
   read (n);
   comment now we define the arrays and the other
           variables needed;
   begin real array X, W [1:n]; real sumwx, sumx, a;
        integer j;
   comment input X values and weights;
   for j := 1 step 1 until n do read (X [j], W [j]);
   comment clear the sums initially;
   sumwx := sumx := 0;
   for j := 1 step 1 until n do
                 begin sumwx := sumwx + X[j] × W [j];
                       sumx := sumx + X [j];
                       comment that brings the sums up to
                                                     date;
                 end;
   comment now compute quotient and print result;
   a := sumwx / sumx;
   print ('RESULT IS  ', a)
   end
end of Algol 60 solution
```

As you will see, although this program has a form which is, in many respects, quite at variance with that of the Fortran programs with which we have previously dealt, the essential features remain unchanged.

One important difference is that Algol makes use of a feature known as *dynamic storage allocation*, the effect of which is that only as much store need be reserved as there is an immediate demand for. This is seen in the early lines of the program, when the array storage is not specified until it is known what the value of *n* (the number of array elements) will be. Also, you will notice, it is necessary to declare *all* variables, and that the comment feature is much more flexible.

The statements which begin:

for *j* := 1 **step** 1 **until** *n* **do** . . .

are the Algol equivalent of Fortran DO statements which might start:

DO 10 J = 1, N

Again, the Algol structure is much more flexible than that of Fortran.

The words **begin** and **end** have rather specialised meanings in Algol: they are used to mark the beginning and ending points of the program, but they can also be used to delimit a group of statements which are to be treated as though they were a single statement. Such a group is called a *compound statement* or, if the symbol **begin** is immediately followed by declarations, a *block*. Every complete program is thus a block, under normal circumstances, and may have other blocks embedded in it. This is a very powerful feature, with many interesting repercussions which, because of the nature of this book, we are not able to pursue here. The interested reader is referred to any of the excellent texts on Algol programming which are currently available.

Algol 60, although at first glance appearing to be very

different from Fortran, functions on very similar basic principles, though it offers its user considerably more computational facilities combined with extreme elegance. Unfortunately, it lacks well-defined standards of input and output, and strong backing from the manufacturers of computing equipment—an area in which Fortran has always held the whip-hand. However, there is now a serious contender for Fortran's position, in the shape of an Algol-like language with features which make it attractive to both the commercial and the scientific user. This language is PL/1.

PL/1 solution

Like Algol, PL/1 has many facets which it is not possible to deal with in the brief space available here. The example given may, however, serve to show the general form of programs written in the language.

```
SUM: PROCEDURE;
       /* INPUT NUMBER OF VALUES */
       GET LIST (N);
       BEGIN;
       /* NOW WE DECLARE THE ARRAYS TO
          BE USED IN TERMS OF THE SPACE
          NEEDED (N ELEMENTS EACH). WE
          ALSO GIVE INITIAL VALUES TO
          CERTAIN VARIABLES—COMPARE
          WITH THE FORTRAN DATA
          STATEMENT */
       DECLARE X(N), W(N), (SUMXW, SUMX)
          INITIAL (0);
       /* INPUT VALUES AND WEIGHTS */
       GET LIST ((X(J), W(J) DO J = 1 TO N));
       /* FORM SUMS OF X AND WEIGHTED
          X */
```

```
        DO J = 1 TO N;
              SUMXW = SUMXW + X(J) * W(J);
              SUMX = SUMX + X(J);
        END;
        /* THAT END TERMINATES THE SET OF
           STATEMENTS CONTROLLED BY THE
           DO */
        /* NEXT WE COMPUTE AND PRINT
           THE QUOTIENT */
        A = SUMXW / SUMX;
        PUT LIST (A);
        END; /* OF THE BEGIN ON LINE 4 */
END SUM;
```

Comments are enclosed between '/*' and '*/', and the layout of the program is, as with Algol, free form—that is, there are no restrictions as to which column on the card any particular field starts in. Only capital letters may be used, but the character set is, in general, larger than that of Fortran.

Lines 3 and 12 illustrate one of several means by which data can be brought into the main memory, and line 22 shows a similar method of output. As in Fortran, if variables are not specifically declared, the system will make assumptions about their types. Line 10 shows X and W being specifically declared as arrays, each having N elements, and in the same line both SUMXW and SUMX are given initial values of zero. No indication of type is given, however, and the system will decide what is intended by reference to a set of 'default' values built in to it. Line 12 also shows a structure similar in appearance and purpose to the implied DO loop of Fortran, for input of a complete array.

The DO loop proper is shown on lines 14 through 17. Note that the word END acts to define the range of the DO.

The program finishes with the word END followed by the name of the routine (or PROCEDURE), which is SUM.

What next?

The brief examples of other programming languages which have been given should have persuaded anyone who has read the rest of this book that, knowing Fortran and the basic principles of programming, he should not experience too much trouble in learning another programming language.

There can be little doubt that some programming languages will become even more specialised and sophisticated than they are at the present time. A great deal of effort is being expended in research on programming languages, and one hopes that they will become not only more powerful but also easier to learn and use, culminating perhaps in the ability to address and instruct machines in languages which are little different from those used in one's normal work.

The dream of having computers which could accept instructions in, say, everyday English has, so far, proved very difficult to realise, since natural languages tend to be ambiguous in their meaning. A number of languages do approximate to the ideal, but the day when one can write programs in even basic English still seems to be out of sight.

Answers to exercises

Chapter 2

1.

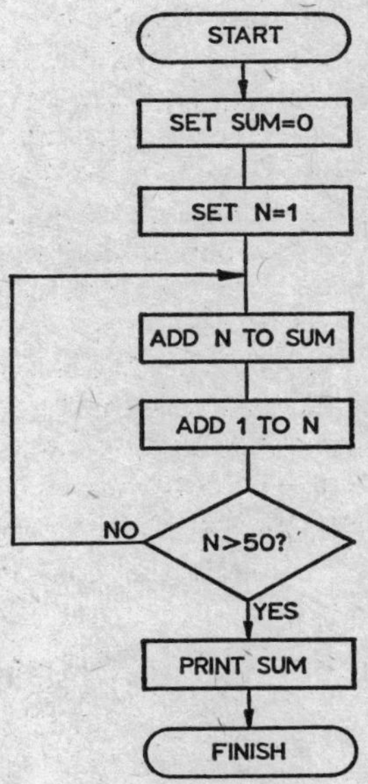

Fig. A1

2.

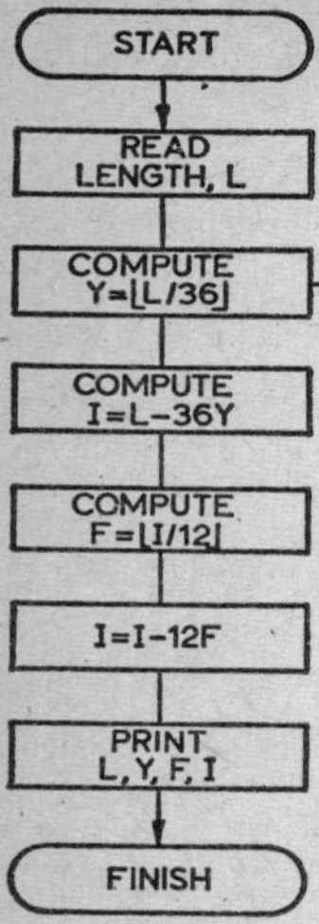

⌊---⌋ means 'the whole-number part of ----'

Fig. A2

3.

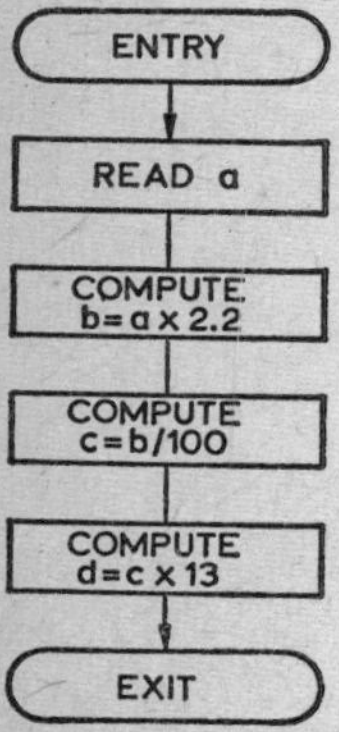

a is the cost in pence/lb

2.2 lb = 1 kg
b is the cost in pence/kg

100p = £1
c is the cost in £/kg

13NF = £1
d is the cost in NF/kg

This is repeated for each item

Fig. A3

4.

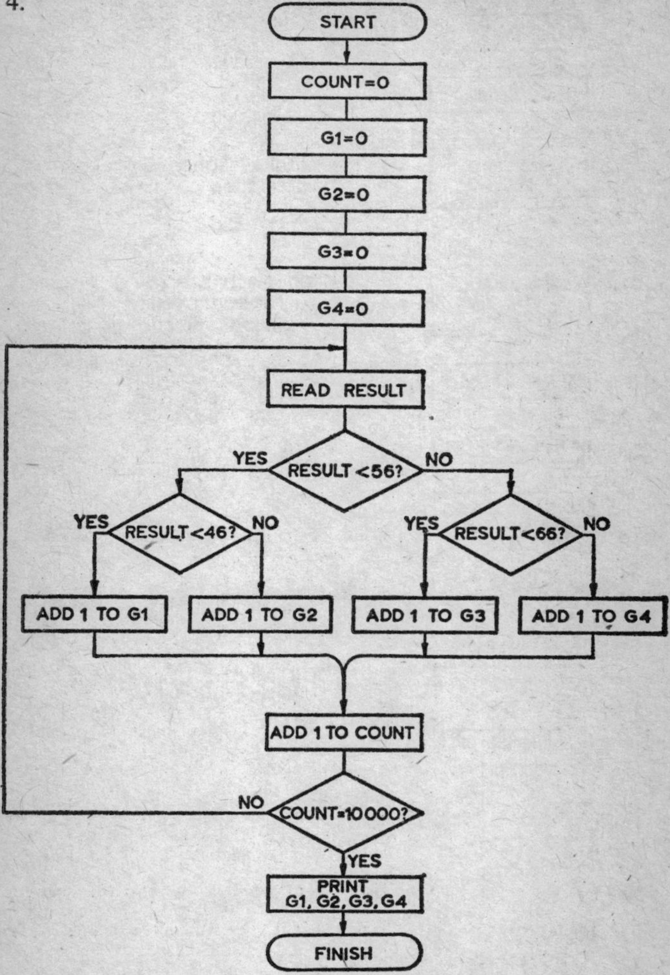
START
COUNT=0
G1=0
G2=0
G3=0
G4=0
READ RESULT
RESULT<56?
YES
NO
RESULT<46?
YES
NO
RESULT<66?
YES
NO
ADD 1 TO G1
ADD 1 TO G2
ADD 1 TO G3
ADD 1 TO G4
ADD 1 TO COUNT
COUNT=10000?
NO
YES
PRINT G1, G2, G3, G4
FINISH

Fig. A4

5.

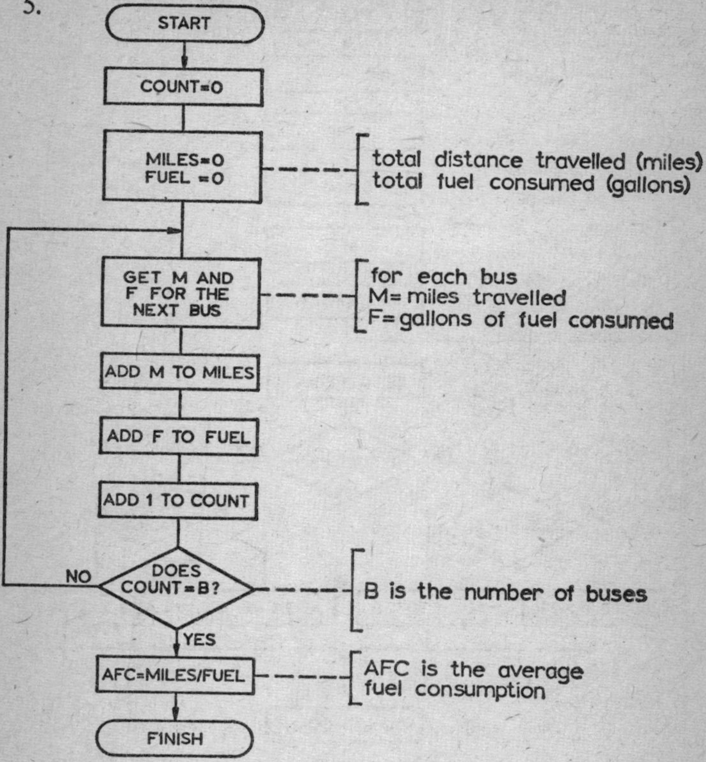

Fig. A5

Chapter 3

1. (*a*) −0.1079E3
   (*b*) 0.397E−2
   (*c*) 0.2522E10

(*d*) −0.196E0
(*e*) 0.3973E1
(*f*) −0.292E4

2. (*a*) 0.000219
(*b*) −0.0000008169
(*c*) 32220.0
(*d*) 0.0213

3. (*a*) correct
(*b*) incorrect—starts with an 'L'
(*c*) incorrect—starts with a digit
(*d*) correct
(*e*) incorrect—too many characters
(*f*) incorrect—starts with a 'K'
(*g*) correct
(*h*) incorrect—contains a special character

4. (*a*) correct
(*b*) incorrect—too many subscripts
(*c*) incorrect—this is real
(*d*) incorrect—subscripts must be integer
(*e*) this one is *syntactically* correct, but will cause a run-time error when the subscript turns out to be negative
(*f*) correct
(*g*) correct
(*h*) incorrect—subscripts must be of integer type
(*i*) incorrect—subscripts should not be subscripted
(*j*) incorrect—too many characters in array name
(*k*) incorrect—no closing parenthesis
(*l*) correct

5. (*a*) (5, 2)
(*b*) (1, 5)
(*c*) (2, 3)
(*d*) stock level of item 3

(*e*) weekly demand of item 4
(*f*) price of item 3

6.
```
DIMENSION A(6, 17), GAIN(3, 4), D(3),
*                   DATE(6, 2, 2)
```

7. (*a*) no commas between array declarations
   (*b*) word 'DIMENSION' wrongly spelt

Chapter 4

1. (*a*) false
   (*b*) false
   (*c*) true
   (*d*) false
   (*e*) false
   (*f*) true

2. (*a*) F(9) = 12.46
   (*b*) P = 6.25
   (*c*) ALPHA = 64.0

3. (*a*) correct
   (*b*) incorrect—A subtracted from 3.9
   (*c*) incorrect—B is raised to power 3
   (*d*) correct
   (*e*) incorrect—L.H.S. must be a single variable
   (*f*) correct
   (*g*) incorrect—parentheses needed around 'A—3.9'

4. E = (3.479*D*P**2)/(5.67+Q)

5. Y = 8.0*X**3 + 7.0*X + 4.3*X**2

6. Y = ((8.0*X + 4.3)*X + 7.0)*X

7. (*a*) 6
   (*b*) 19.0
   (*c*) 5.0
   (*d*) 0.25

8. K = 13

9. (*a*) mixed modes
   (*b*) parentheses do not balance, and mixed mode ('8' should be '8.0')
   (*c*) L.H.S. is incorrectly formed
   (*d*) 'CALCULATION' is not a valid variable name
   (*e*) two operators (+ and *) may not be adjacent in an expression

10. $$kk_3 = \frac{2\,(mn_5{}^2 - n_4)}{n_4}$$

Chapter 5

1. (*a*) false
   (*b*) true
   (*c*) false
   (*d*) true
   (*e*) false—a subscripted control variable is not allowed

2. (*a*)

```
      K = KA(19)-453
      GO TO (12, 13, 14, 15), K
```

(*b*)

```
      IF (KA(19)-455) 12, 13, 16
   16 IF (KA(19)-457) 14, 15, 15
```

(*c*)

```
      K = KA(19)
      IF (K .EQ. 454) GO TO 12
      IF (K .EQ. 455) GO TO 13
      IF (K .EQ. 456) GO TO 14
      GO TO 15
```

3. (*a*) no comma needed after '34', and initial value must not be negative
   (*b*) DO parameters may not be subscripted
   (*c*) DO parameters must be of integer type
   (*d*) control variable must be of integer type

4. (*a*) no comma required after the closing parenthesis, and the third label is missing
   (*b*) missing right parenthesis
   (*c*) only three statement numbers permitted
   (*d*) mixed mode in parenthesised expression
   (*e*) not strictly wrong, but the statement refers to itself, and may induce an inescapable loop

5. (*a*)
```
      IF (DS(17)) 1, 2, 1
```
(*b*)
```
      IF (B(9, 7)) 3, 3, 2
    3 IF (T(9)) 2, 1, 2
```
(*c*)
```
      GO TO (3, 3, 3, 2, 2), K
    3 IF (A(4)) 1, 1, 2
```
(*d*)
```
      IF (T**2 - V**3) 2, 3, 2
    3 IF (T - S) 1, 2, 1
```
(*e*)
```
      IF (C - D) 3, 2, 3
    3 IF (C - E) 4, 2, 4
    4 IF (C - F) 5, 2, 5
    5 IF (C - G) 1, 2, 1
```

6.
```
      DO 1 J = 1, 10
      DO 1 K = 1, 10
         M = MAT(K, J)
         MATX(J, K) = M*M
    1 CONTINUE
      . . .
```

7.
```
      SUM = 0.0
      DO 1 J = 1, 30
         SUM = SUM + A(J)*B(J)
```

```
    1 CONTINUE
      IF (SUM - 3050.0) 45, 45, 56
or
      IF (SUM .GT. 3050.0) GO TO 56
   45 CONTINUE
      . . .
```

Chapter 6

1. (*a*) correct
   (*b*) correct
   (*c*) incorrect—attempt to read on output device
   (*d*) incorrect—no commas between variable names
   (*e*) incorrect—no comma required after READ
   (*f*) incorrect—statement numbers must be unsigned
   (*g*) incorrect—all variables in the list must be unsigned
   (*h*) correct
   (*i*) incorrect—missing parentheses. Should be:

   ```
      READ (3, 999) (RESULT(J), J = 1, 10)
   ```

   (*j*) correct

2.
```
      READ(2, 35) ((TURN(I, J), J = 1, 4), I = 1, 30)
   35 FORMAT(2F9.4)
```

3. (*a*) incorrect—no statement number
   (*b*) incorrect—F9.12 is invalid
   (*c*) correct
   (*d*) correct
   (*e*) incorrect—requires 240 columns, too many for normal input/output device
   (*f*) incorrect—Hollerith constant should be '7H . . .'
   (*g*) incorrect—parentheses are unbalanced
   (*h*) correct
   (*i*) incorrect—missing left parenthesis
   (*j*) incorrect—F9.9 is invalid

4.
```
      WRITE (3, 7)
    7 FORMAT(50X, 20HUPDATED STOCK RECORD//
     *          55X, 11HCITY  BRANCH)
```

5.
```
      READ(2, 35) ((TURN(I, J), I = 1, 30), J = 1, 4)
   35 FORMAT(2F9.4)
```

6.
```
      WRITE(3, 8) SUM, DIFF, LIM
      WRITE(4, 8) SUM, DIFF, LIM
    8 FORMAT (6X, F8.2, 5X, F8.2, 5X, I6)
```

7. Change the FORMAT statement thus:

```
    8 FORMAT(6X, F8.2 / 6X, F8.2 / 6X, I6)
```

8.
```
      READ(2, 3) (ALPHA(I), I = 1, 4)
    3 FORMAT(4A5)
```

9. (*a*) false
   (*b*) false
   (*c*) true
   (*d*) false
   (*e*) true
   (*f*) false
   (*g*) true
   (*h*) false

Chapter 7

1.
```
C * AVHT    = AVERAGE HEIGHT OF
C             CHILDREN AGED 5 TO 7
C * AVWT    = AVERAGE WEIGHT OF
C             CHILDREN OVER 125 CM TALL
C * NCHILD  = NUMBER OF CHILDREN
C             AGED OVER 7 YEARS
```

```
C * N57      = NUMBER OF CHILDREN
C              AGED 5 TO 7
C * NO125    = NUMBER OF CHILDREN
C              OVER 125 CM TALL
C
C * INITIALISE
C
    AVHT     = 0.0
    AVWT     = 0.0
    N57      = 0
    NO125    = 0
    NCHILD   = 0
C
C * MAIN LOOP
C
    DO 30 I = 1, 1400
        READ(2, 100) AGE, HEIGHT, WEIGHT
 100    FORMAT(3F7.0)
        IF (AGE .LE. 7.0) GO TO 10
C * COUNT OVER - 7 S
        NCHILD = NCHILD + 1
        GO TO 20
  10    IF (AGE .LT. 5.0) GO TO 20
C * 5 - TO - 7 S - ACCUMULATE HEIGHTS
        N57 = N57 + 1
        AVHT = AVHT + HEIGHT
  20    IF (HEIGHT .LE. 125.0) GO TO 30
C * OVER 125 CM - ACCUMULATE WEIGHTS
        AVWT = AVWT + WEIGHT
        NO125 = NO125 + 1
 30 CONTINUE
C
C * COMPUTE AVERAGES
C * FIRST, FLOAT NO125 and N57
C
    FNO125 = NO125
```

```
      FN57 = N57
      AVWT = AVWT/FNO125
      AVHT = AVHT/FN57
      WRITE(3, 200) AVHT, NCHILD, AVWT
  200 FORMAT(10X, 15HAVERAGE HEIGHT,,
     *               15H AGES 5 TO 7 = , F9.2/
     *          10X, 16HNUMBER AGED OVER,
     *               14H 7          = , I4/
     *          10X, 15HAVERAGE WEIGHT,,
     *               15H OVER 125 CM = , F9.2)
C
C * THE SHORT LINES, AND HENCE
C * CONTINUATIONS, DIRECTLY REFLECT
C * THE PAGE SIZE
C
      CALL EXIT
      END
```

2.

```
      DIMENSION DATA (1000)
      READ(2, 100) N
  100 FORMAT(I3)
      READ(2, 200) (DATA(I), I = 1, N)
  200 FORMAT(5(F12.0, 4X))
      SMALL = 100.0
      DO 10 I = 1, N
         IF (X(I) .LT. SMALL) SMALL = X(I)
   10 CONTINUE
      WRITE(3, 300) SMALL
      FORMAT(10X, 18HSMALLEST VALUE IS ,
     *  F12.6)
      CALL EXIT
      END
```

3.

```
      IPAGE = 0
C * ENSURE THAT WE START ON A NEW PAGE
      LINE = 100
```

```
C * ENSURE THAT THE LINE COUNT IS
C * PROPERLY SET UP THE FIRST TIME ROUND
       DO 20 IX = 1, 150
          IF (LINE .LT. 25) GO TO 10
          LINE = 0
          IPAGE = IPAGE + 1
C * OUTPUT OF HEADINGS ON EVERY PAGE
          WRITE(3, 100) IPAGE
  100     FORMAT(1H1, 100X, 4HPAGE, I2/
     *    1H0, 52X, 1HX, 5X, 9HX SQUARED)
   10     IXSQ = IX * IX
          WRITE(3, 200) IX, IXSQ
  200     FORMAT(1H0, 51X, I3, 5X, I6)
   20  CONTINUE
       CALL EXIT
       END
```

4.

```
       DIMENSION XVAL(45), IVAL(45)
       EQUIVALENCE (XVAL(1), IVAL(1))
       DO 10 I = 1, 45
   10  IVAL(I) = XVAL(I)
```

5. (*a*) the comma after 'EQUIVALENCE' must be removed
   (*b*) variables to be equivalenced must be enclosed in parentheses

Chapter 8

3. A statement function will be used, since the result is a single value and the calculation is expressible in a single statement:

```
      F(T, U, V) = T*T + U**3 + V**4
```

4. COT = COS(ANGLE*0.01745)/SIN(ANGLE*0·01745)

On the whole, it is probably not advisable to code this as a single statement, since it involves the evaluation of the expression

ANGLE*0.01745

twice. The following would probably be a better approach:

```
RANGLE = ANGLE*0.01745
COT = COS(RANGLE)/SIN(RANGLE)
```

0.01745 is, of course, the constant for conversion from degrees to radian measure, which the trigonometric functions require.

5.

```
      SUBROUTINE ADDUP
      COMMON WEEK(7)
      A = 0.0
      DO 10 I = 1, 7
   10 A = A + WEEK(I)
      WEEK(1) = A/7.0
      RETURN
      END
```

The calling statement will be:

```
      CALL ADDUP
```

6. This is not so easy as it seems, when X, Y and Z are real variables. The reason is that the difference between two floating-point numbers, calculated by different instruction sequences but representing the same value, may not be exactly zero. The difference will be small but may be sufficient to invalidate a test for zero. We may thus have to decide what is a small enough difference, for our

purpose, to be *regarded as* zero. Here we choose 1.0E-6 (i.e. $1 * 10^{-6}$).

```
      FUNCTION COMP(X, Y, Z)
      IF (ABS(X – Y) .GT. 1.0E – 6) GO TO 1
    2 COMP = 3.0
      GO TO 10
    1 IF (ABS(X – Z) .GT. 1.0E – 6) GO TO 3
    4 COMP = 4.0
      GO TO 10
    3 COMP = 6.0
   10 RETURN
      END
```

Each 'GO TO 10' could be replaced by 'RETURN', but it is considered by many to be good programming practice to have but one exit point from a subprogram.

7. (*a*) true
   (*b*) false
   (*c*) false
   (*d*) true
   (*e*) false
   (*f*) false

8. (*a*) no commas between the arguments
   (*b*) dummy variables do not appear in the defined statement
   (*c*) unbalanced parentheses
   (*d*) illegal subroutine name—too many characters
   (*e*) dummy variables should not be subscripted

Chapter 9

1.
```
      INTEGER ANT, Y, XRETY, STEREO, QUADRO,
     *                D7, E2R, PIN
```

   All the rest are already of integer type.

2.
```
      LOGICAL Z
      Z = X .GT. Y
```

3. (*a*) A may take only the values .TRUE. and .FALSE.
   (*b*) mixed mode—J has not been declared REAL
   (*c*) nothing is wrong, but since ARTHUR is the name of a real variable, the 'REAL' is redundant
   (*d*) confusion between logical and arithmetic IFs
   (*e*) OA should have been declared LOGICAL if it is to have a logical value assigned to it

Index

TEACH YOURSELF BOOKS

ELECTRONIC COMPUTERS

F. L. Westwater

Electronic computers and computer technology are becoming increasingly part of our everyday lives. If there has been any technological revolution in the past few years, it has been in this field.

This book explains, with the help of illustrations, the use, principles and functions of digital computers. It is designed as a basic introduction to the complex subject of electronic computers and as such it will be of interest to those readers embarking on a career in computers, as well as to readers who come into contact with computers, either in business or through their many applications in everyday life, and who feel they want to learn more about computers.

Fully revised and updated, by an expert in the computer field, this book will be of interest to the specialist and interested layman alike.

United Kingdom	40p
Australia (recommended)	$1.25
New Zealand	$1.10
Canada	$1.50

ISBN 0 340 09702 7

Available wherever Teach Yourself Books are sold

TEACH YOURSELF BOOKS

CYBERNETICS

F. H. George

This book is an introductory outline to the ramifications of the science called 'Cybernetics', a science concerned with all matters of control and communication.

Cybernetics covers both the pure theory of the science—mathematical, statistical and logical—and its application, which affects everything that human beings do—especially how to learn, make decisions, plan and solve problems, in such fields as Engineering, Management and Education. The author, Director of the Institute of Cybernetics at Brunel University, has been careful to write this general introduction in language intelligible to the layman.

United Kingdom	40p
Australia (recommended)	$1.25
New Zealand	$1.10
Canada	$1.50

ISBN 0 340 05941 9

Available wherever Teach Yourself Books are sold

TEACH YOURSELF BOOKS

CRITICAL PATH ANALYSIS

D. W. Lang

This comprehensive introduction to the increasingly important field of Critical Path Analysis has been developed from experience in consultancy and teaching.

It provides the basic knowledge necessary for the application of systematic reasoning to the planning and controlling of practical situations consisting of many separate, and often simultaneous, jobs.

Illustrations, exercises and case studies enable the reader to apply the technique successfully and to appreciate the practical aspects of the subject.

United Kingdom	40p
Australia (recommended)	$1.25
New Zealand	$1.10
Canada	$1.50

ISBN 0 340 11450 9

Available wherever Teach Yourself Books are sold